Avenues

Alfredo Schifini
Deborah J. Short
Josefina Villamil Tinajero

Erminda García
Eugene E. García
Else Hamayan
Lada Kratky

HAMPTON-BROWN

Grades 1–2 Curriculum Reviewers

Acknowledgments

Every effort has been made to secure permission, but if any omissions have been made, please let us know. We gratefully acknowledge the following permissions:

Cover Design and Art Direction: Pronk&Associates.

Cover Illustration: Anna-Liisa Hakkarainen.

Children's Book Press: *A Movie in My Pillow* by Jorge Argueta. Reprinted with the permission of the publisher, Children's Book Press, San Francisco, CA. Poems copyright © 2001 by Jorge Argueta. Illustrations copyright © 2001 by Elizabeth Gómez.

Acknowledgments continue on page 420.

Hampton-Brown
P.O. Box 223220
Carmel, California 93922
800-333-3510
www.hampton-brown.com

Printed in the United States of America

ISBN 0-7362-1876-9

04 05 06 07 08 09 10 11 12 9 8 7 6 5 4 3 2

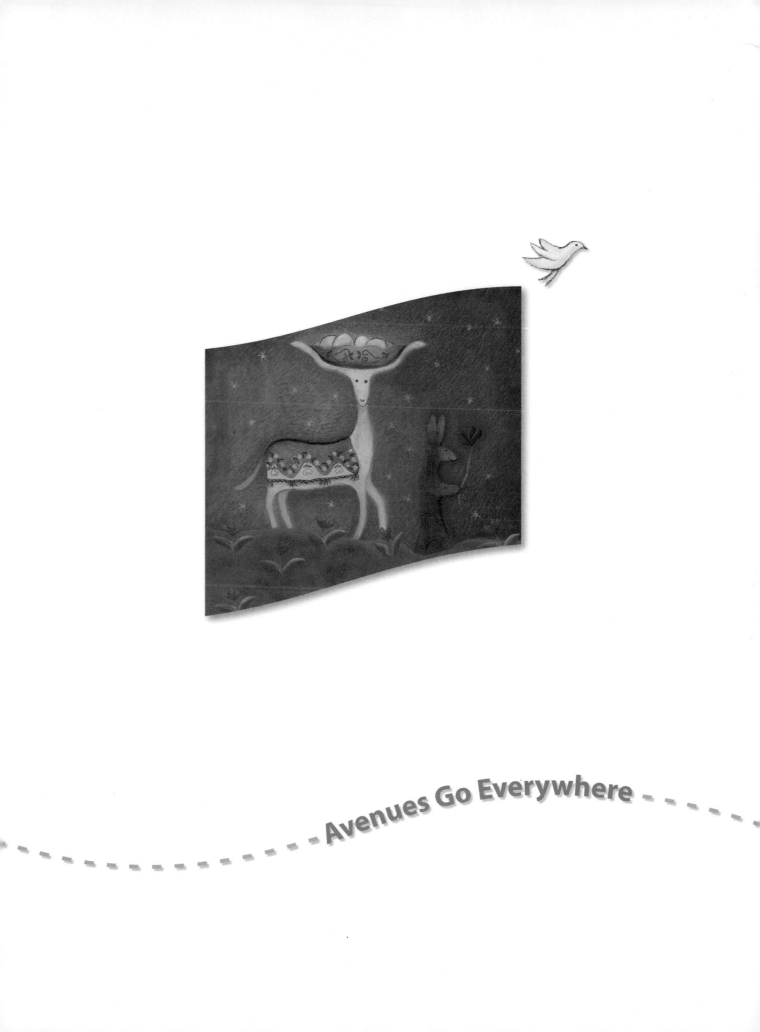

Avenues Go Everywhere

Unit 1 The **Big** City

Social Studies
- Urban Communities
- Geography

Unit

2

Seed to
Sandwich

Social Studies
■ Economics
■ Farming

Unit 3

Water, Water, Everywhere

Science
- Water Cycle

Social Studies
- Geography

Social Studies
- Celebrations
- U.S. History

Unit 5

Catch Me If You Can

Science
- Animal Adaptations
- Animal Classification

Nonfiction
Science Article

What Do You Do When Something Wants To Eat You?
by Steve Jenkins

Fiction
Animal Fantasy

Grandpa Toad's Secrets
by Keiko Kasza

Unit
6

Make Some NOISE!

Science
- Sound

The Big City

Make a City Picture Frame

1. Make a tall building.
2. Put a picture of your face in one of the windows.
3. Put your building with your classmates' buildings.

Social Studies Words

City Places

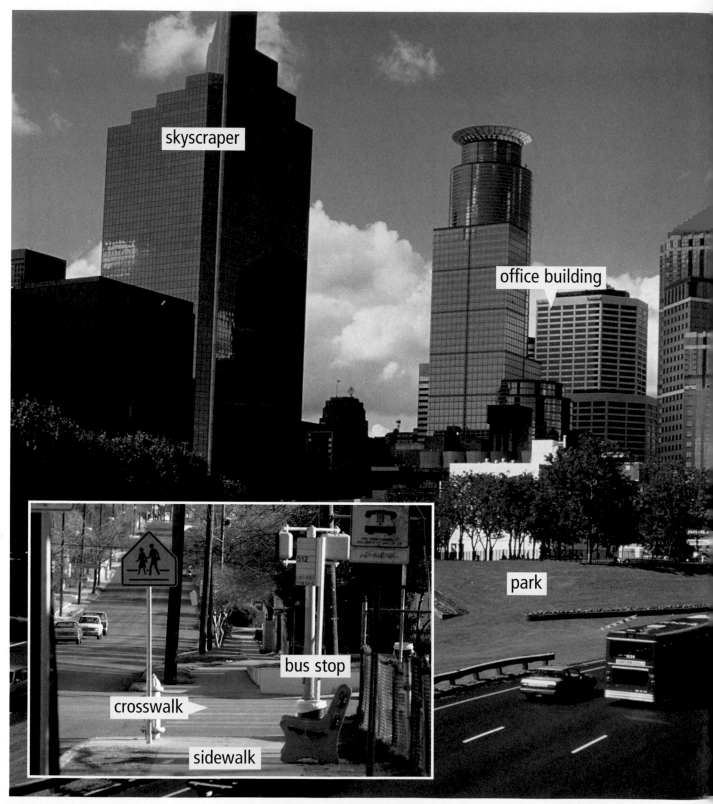

skyscraper

office building

park

crosswalk

bus stop

sidewalk

Transportation

apartment building

street

taxi

bus

subway

delivery truck

Song

My New Neighborhood

I **left** friends **behind**

In my old **neighborhood** .

But when I **arrived**

In my new neighborhood,

Children **everywhere**

Smiled at me

Because they were friendly

Just like me!

—Evelyn Stone

Tune: "Mi chacra"

14

Key Words

left

behind

neighborhood

arrive

everywhere

Read Poems

A **poem** tells about feelings and ideas in a special way. These poems tell a true story about the poet's life.

✔ Look for the **title** of each poem. It tells what the poem is mostly about.

title

Wonders of the City

Here in the city there are **wonders** everywhere

Selection Reading

Poems from
A Movie in My Pillow

by Jorge Argueta
illustrated by Elizabeth Gómez

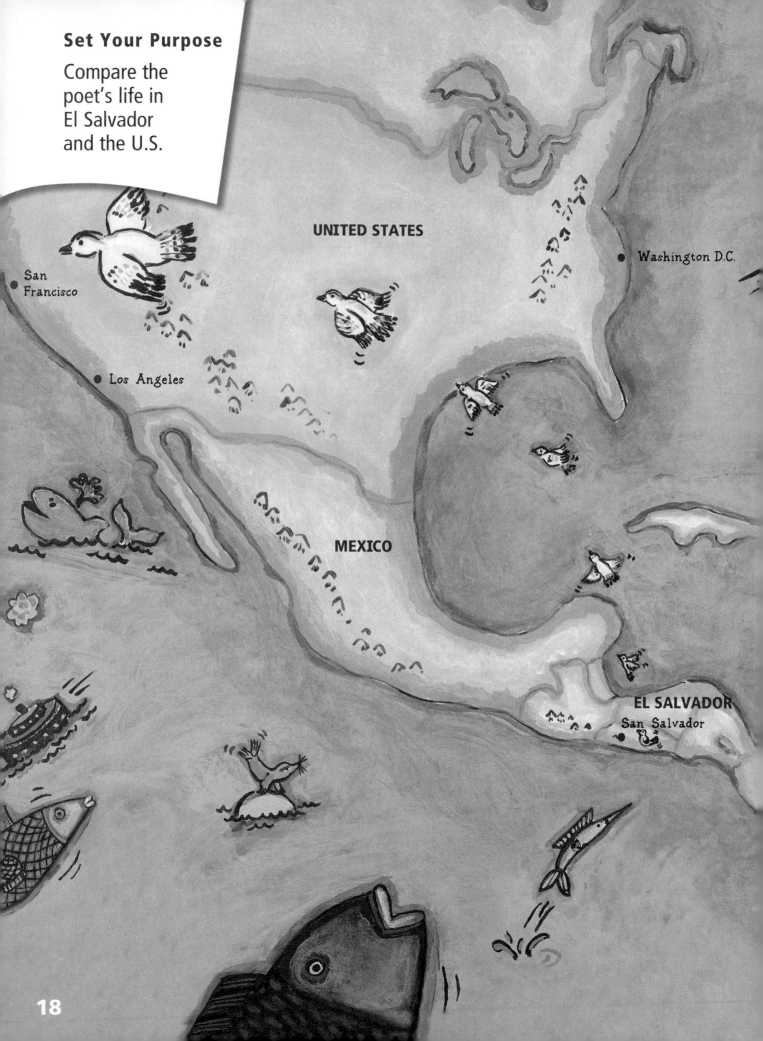

UNITED STATES

San Francisco

Los Angeles

Washington D.C.

MEXICO

EL SALVADOR

San Salvador

These poems are based on my life when I first came to this country. These poems are my memories, my dreams—the movies in my pillow. I dedicate them to all the children from El Salvador—and to children **everywhere** —with the hope that we may all have a beautiful tomorrow.

—Jorge Argueta

Table of Contents

Neighborhood of Sun

I live in San Francisco
in the Mission District
Neighborhood of sun
of colors and flavors

Avocadoes and mangoes
papayas and watermelons
Here my friend Tomás
laughs louder with the sun

Here in my neighborhood
you can **taste**

a soup of languages
in the wind

———————————

taste a soup of languages in the wind
hear many different languages

Chinese in the restaurant
Arabic in the grocery store
and everywhere
English and Spanish

Here in my **barrio**
the Mission District
the sun always shines
just like in El Salvador

---

barrio neighborhood
(in Spanish)

Before You Move On
1. **Details** Where does the poet live now? Where did he come from?
2. **Conclusion** What is the Mission District like?

When We Left El Salvador

When we **left** El Salvador
to come to the United States
Papa and I left **in a hurry**
one early morning in December

We left without saying goodbye
to **relatives**, friends, or neighbors
I didn't say goodbye to Neto
my best friend

---

in a hurry quickly
relatives people in our family

I didn't say goodbye to Koki
my happy talking **parakeet**
I didn't say goodbye to
Miss Sha-Sha-She-Sha
my very dear **doggie**

———————————

parakeet bird
doggie dog

When we left El Salvador
in a bus I couldn't stop crying
because I had **left** my mama
my little brothers and my
grandma **behind**

Before You Move On

1. **Cause/Effect** Why does the poet cry?

2. **Comparison** Compare how the poet feels in the two poems you read.

27

Wonders of the City

Here in the city there are
wonders everywhere

Here mangoes
come in cans

In El Salvador
they grew on trees

Here chickens come
in plastic bags

Over there
they slept beside me

_____

wonders strange, good things

Language of the Birds

I used to speak
only Spanish

Now I can speak
English too

And in my dreams
I speak in Nahuatl

the language
my grandma says

her people—
the Pipiles—

learned
from the birds

---

the Pipiles a group of people
from El Salvador

Before You Move On

1. **Comparison** Tell how
   life in El Salvador is
   different from life here.
2. **Inference** Why can the
   poet speak English now?

Family Nest

Today my mama
and my little brothers
arrived from El Salvador

I **hardly recognize them**
but when we hug each other
we feel like a big nest
with all the birds inside

_____

hardly recognize them almost
forgot what they look like

Before You Move On
1. **Summarize** Tell what happens in this poem.
2. **Cause/Effect** How does hugging his family make the poet feel? Why?

A Band of Parakeets

Every Saturday morning
Mama and Papa
my little brothers
and I walk
on 24th Street

We are like a **band**
of parakeets flying
from San Francisco
to El Salvador
and back again

---

band group

Before You Move On

1. **Poetic Language** Does the poet really fly? What does he mean?

2. **Conclusion** Is the poet happy now? Explain.

Think and Respond

Strategy: Make Comparisons

Make a Venn diagram. Compare the poet's life in El Salvador to his life in the United States.

A Movie in My Pillow

Tell about one place here.

Tell about the other place here.

El Salvador

mangoes on trees

Both

sunshine

United States

mangoes in cans

Tell how both places are the same here.

Ask and Answer Questions

Work with a partner. Use your completed diagram. One partner pretends to be Jorge Argueta, the poet. The other asks questions about his life.

Talk It Over

1 **Personal Response** How do the poems make you feel? Why?

2 **Judgment** Are friends and family important to the author? How do you know?

3 **Author's Purpose** Why do you think the poet wrote these poems?

Compare Themes

"A Movie in My Pillow" is about a family. Compare these poems to other stories you know about families.

Content Connections

Play a Game

Pretend you move to a new city. What will you take with you? Share your ideas with the class.

I will take books and clothes.

large group

Make a City Postcard

Internet

partners

1. Find a picture of a U.S. city on the Internet.

2. Print the picture.

3. Write a caption.

4. Put the picture on a U.S. map.

Seattle is a city in Washington.

Make a Display

What is your neighborhood like? Take a walk. What do you see? Make a model.

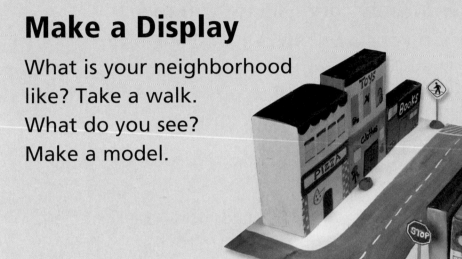

Write a Neighborhood Poem

What is your neighborhood like? Write a poem to tell about it. Choose words that help your reader "see" what things look like.

> My street is
> like a snake.
> It goes around
> the whole city.

Draw Conclusions

When you read and **draw conclusions**, you can figure out things on your own. To draw a conclusion:

✔ Think about details in the story.
✔ Put the details together with what you already know.

Try the strategy.

from

Neighborhood of Sun

Here in my barrio
the Mission District
the sun always shines
just like in El Salvador

> The writer says the weather in the barrio is sunny. I know that "just like" means "the same." So it must also be sunny in El Salvador.

Practice

Take this test and **draw conclusions** about "A Movie in My Pillow."

Test Strategy

Read the directions carefully.

Read each question. Choose the best answer.

1 **Which detail helps you draw this conclusion: The writer feels sad when he leaves El Salvador.**

   ○ He can't stop crying.

   ○ He leaves in December.

   ○ His dog's name is Sha-Sha-She-Sha.

   ○ He comes to the United States with his papa.

2 **The poet hardly recognizes his family when they come from El Salvador. Why?**

   ○ They wore hats.

   ○ Their plane was late.

   ○ He did not know that they were coming.

   ○ He did not see them for a very long time.

CHINATOWN

written and illustrated
by William Low

Read a Story

Genre

This story tells about things that could really happen. It is **realistic fiction**. In the story, a boy and his grandmother walk in their neighborhood.

Characters

boy

grandmother

Setting

This story happens in Chinatown, in New York City.

Selection Reading

1

What do the boy and his grandmother see in Chinatown?

CHINESE AMERICAN

張 中西 杂

I live in Chinatown with my mother, father, and grandmother.

Our **apartment** is above the Chinese
American **grocery store**.

---

apartment home
grocery store store that sells food

Every morning Grandma and I go for a walk through Chinatown. We hold hands before we **cross** the street.

_____

cross go to the other side of

"Watch out for cars, Grandma," I tell her.

Most days the **tai chi** class has already begun by the time we get to the park. Students, young and old, move in the sunlight like **graceful** dancers.

---

tai chi Chinese exercise
graceful good

We always stop and say hello to Mr. Wong, the **street cobbler**. If our shoes need fixing, Mr. Wong can do the job.

"Just like new, and at a good price, too," says Mr. Wong.

---

street cobbler person who works outside, on the sidewalk, to fix shoes

Before You Move On

1. **Details** Where does the boy live?
2. **Setting** What do you know about Chinatown so far?

Find out what
happens
when
Chinatown
gets busy.

Chinatown really **wakes up** when the
delivery trucks arrive.

---

wakes up gets busy

Men with handcarts move quickly over
the sidewalks and into the stores.

Every day Grandma and I walk past the Dai-Dai Restaurant. Roasted chicken is my **favorite**, but Grandma likes duck best.

Sometimes Grandma and I go for lunch at a seafood **restaurant**. I like to watch the fish swim in the tank. Grandma says, "You won't find fresher fish than those in Chinatown."

The kitchen in the restaurant is a **noisy**
place. Hot oil sizzles, vegetables crackle,
and **woks** clang and bang.

---

woks pans

The cooks **shout to be heard**.

---

shout to be heard yell

At the outdoor market **I can barely** move.

_____

I can barely it is hard to

But we go there because
Grandma likes to **buy** fresh
snapping crabs for dinner.

Before You Move On

1. **Viewing** What happens in Chinatown in the morning?
2. **Cause/Effect** Why is the restaurant so noisy?

3 Find out what happens on the boy's favorite holiday.

My favorite **holiday** is Chinese New Year. During the celebrations the streets of Chinatown are always **crowded** .

"Be sure to stay close by," Grandma says.

The New Year's Day parade winds
noisily through the streets.

The New Year's Day parade winds
People dress in special clothes and move

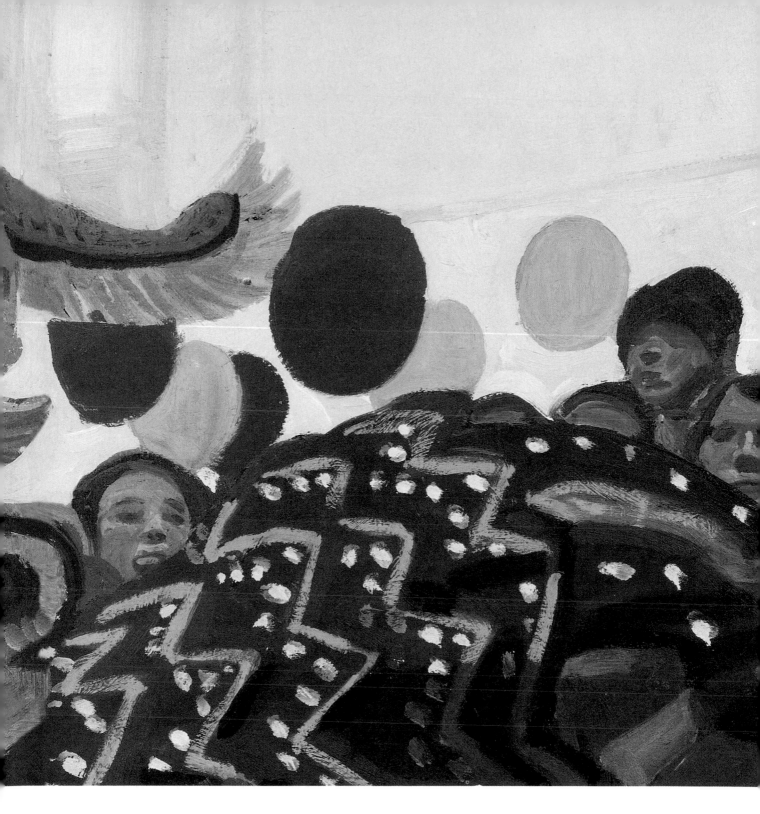

"Look, Grandma!" I say. "Here comes the lion."

Firecrackers **explode** when the lion dance is over. I turn to Grandma, **take** her hand, and say, "***Gung hay fat choy***, Grandma."

She smiles at me. "And a happy new year to you, too."

---

explode make noise
take hold
Gung hay fat choy Happy New Year (in Chinese)

Before You Move On
Personal Experience
Is your neighborhood like Chinatown? Explain.

Meet the Author and Illustrator

William Low

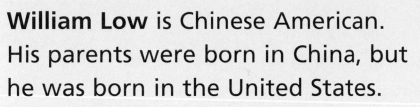

AWARD WINNER

William Low is Chinese American. His parents were born in China, but he was born in the United States.

One day Mr. Low painted a picture of his neighborhood in New York City. It was printed in a newspaper. Since then, Mr. Low has worked as an illustrator.

City

In the morning the city
Spreads its wings
Making a song
In stone that sings.

In the evening the city
Goes to bed
Hanging lights
About its head.

—Langston Hughes

Meet the Poet

Langston Hughes was a very important African American poet. He also wrote books and plays. Mr. Hughes wrote about what he saw.

Before You Move On

Figurative Language
Does the city really have wings? What do you think the author means?

Think and Respond

Strategy: Identify Setting

The setting is where a story happens.
Look for:

✔ names of places

✔ what happens in those places.

Make a setting chart for "Chinatown."

Show the places and what happens there.

Places in Chinatown	What happens there?
apartment	The boy lives with his family.
grocery store	

Draw Conclusions

Would the story be different if it was not in Chinatown? How? Find parts of the story that help you know.

Talk It Over

 Personal Response Do the illustrations make you want to visit Chinatown? Why or why not?

 Conclusion Do you think the boy and the grandmother like being together? Why or why not?

3 **Generalization** Cities are usually crowded. What else can you say about cities?

Compare Ideas

What do *The Adventures of Taxi Dog* and "Chinatown" tell you about cities?

Both tell me that there are many things to see in a city.

Content Connections

Play a Map Game

partners

Look at your map. Choose a place, but do not tell your partner. Give directions to the place you chose. Then ask, "Where are you?" Did your partner find the right place?

I am at the library.

MATH

Restaurant Role-Play

partners

Pretend you are at a restaurant. You have $10. Order food from the menu. Add the prices of your order. How much change do you get?

Have a Job Fair

Internet

1. Research a city worker.

2. Make a poster.

3. Show your poster at a job fair.

4. Decide which job you like best.

badge

phone

Police Officer

Write a Letter

Write a letter to someone in another town. Tell about your town and ask about their town. Send your letter in the mail or by e-mail.

Natasha Borno
656 Maple
Detroit, MI 48201

Emily Kenge
750 Sheridan
Chicago, IL 60645

Plural Nouns

Listen and sing.

Song

The Busy City

We love the big city,

Where shops are so pretty.

We watch all the cars

And the buses go by.

We sit on park benches,

Eat lunches from boxes,

And watch as the shoppers

Go hurrying by.

—Joyce McGreevy

Tune: "Cockles and Mussels"

How Language Works

Plural nouns show more than one thing.

How to Make a Noun Plural	Examples
1. Add **–s** to most nouns.	street street**s**
2. Add **–es** to nouns that end in **x**, **ch**, **sh**, **s**, or **z**.	glass glass**es**

Practice with a Partner

Make each red noun plural. Then say the sentence.

thing   **1.** I see many _____ in the city.

car   **2.** I see big buses and _____ .

box   **3.** I see a market with _____ of fruit.

peach   **4.** I buy some _____ .

Put It in Writing!

Pretend that you go to a store. Tell about the things you see.

I see bunches of grapes.

Show What You Know

Talk About Cities

Look back at the pictures in the unit. Which one is the most interesting? Tell your group why you feel this way.

Make a Mind Map

Show what you learned about cities.

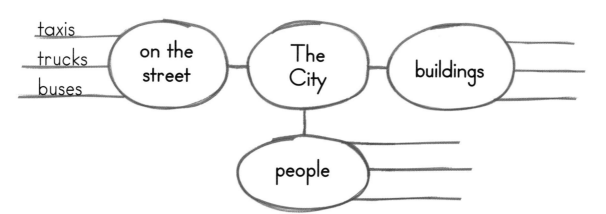

Think and Write

Write about a place in a city that you would like to visit. Tell why. Add this writing to your portfolio.

Read and Learn More

Leveled Books

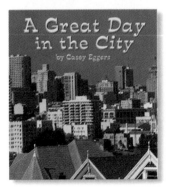

A Great Day in the City
by Casey Eggers

Sing a Song of People
by Lois Lenski

Theme Library

The Rain Came Down
by David Shannon

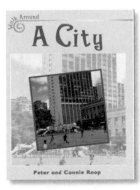

Walk Around A City
by Peter and Connie Roop

Internet

Go to: www.hbavenues.com

Make a Town

Fire Truck Facts

City Workers

Seed to Sandwich

Make Lunch

1. Make a picture of your lunch.
2. Name the foods.
3. Tell where one of the foods comes from.

From Seed to Ketchup

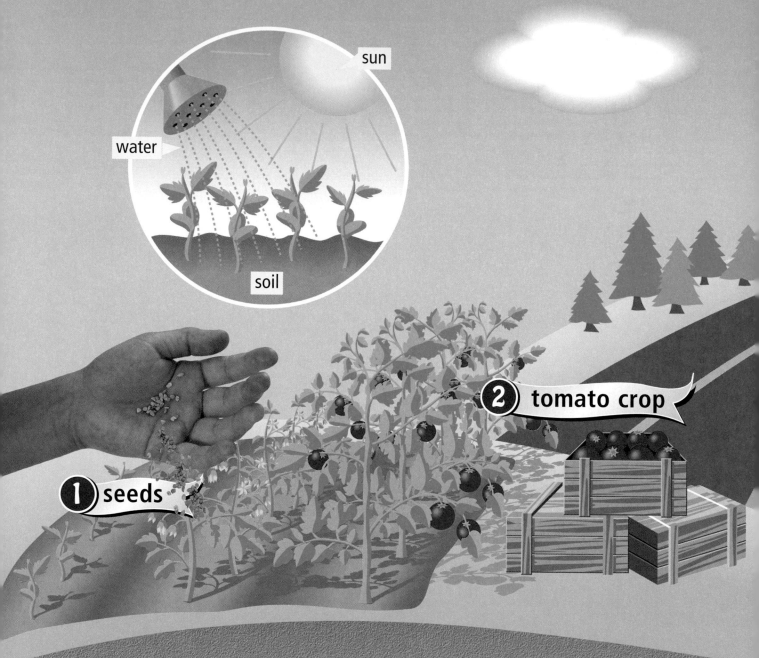

sun

water

soil

1 seeds

2 tomato crop

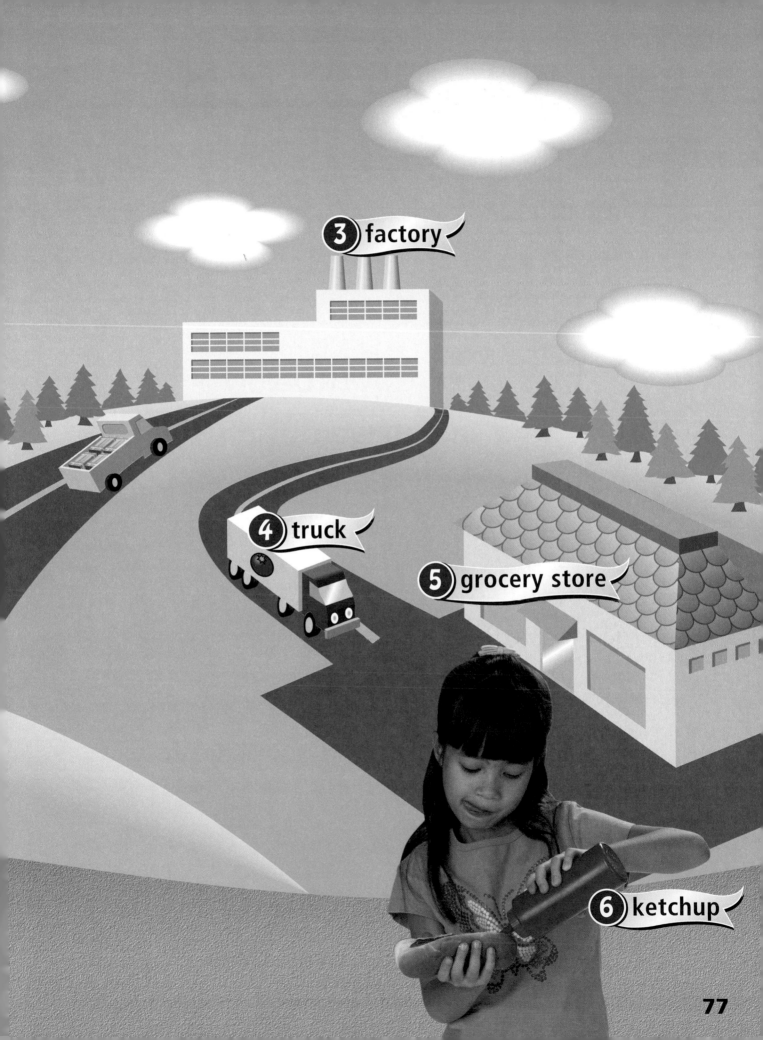

3 factory

4 truck

5 grocery store

6 ketchup

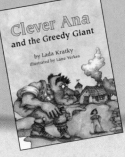
Song

Riddle Song

Roots **grow** down **below**

and **in between** each row.

Above the **ground**

the fruit is growing sweet.

Which part of the tree

is good to eat?

Clever children always know.

—Joyce McGreevy

Tune: "Thumbkin Says"

78

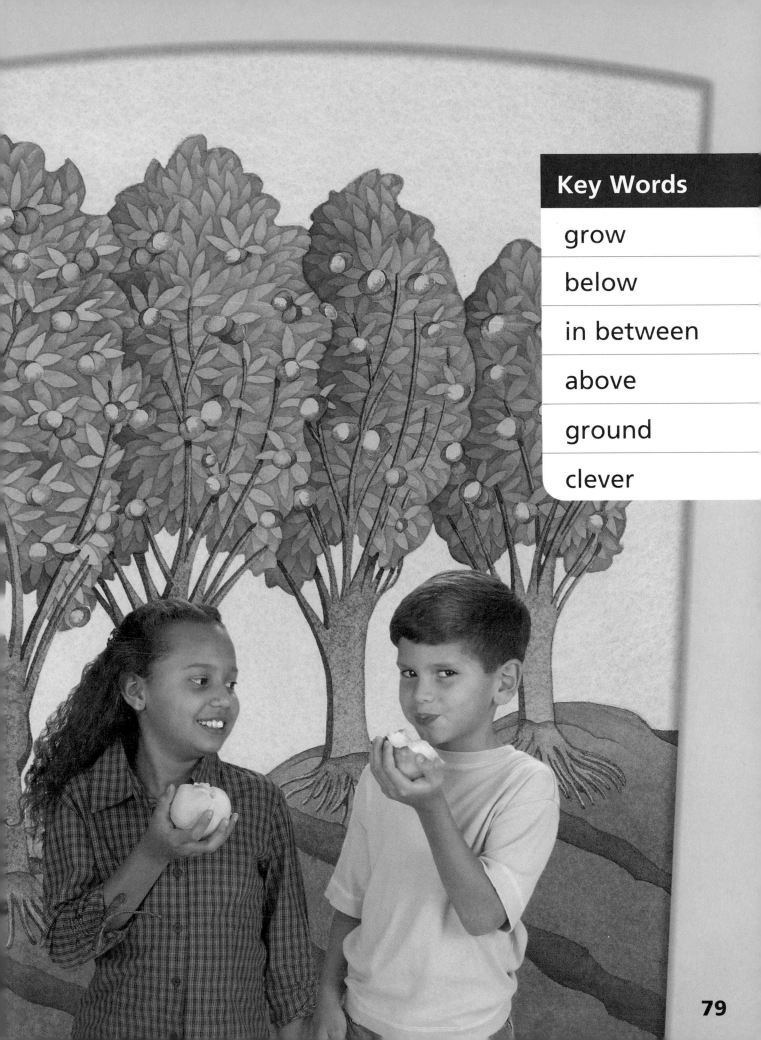

Key Words

grow

below

in between

above

ground

clever

Clever Ana
and the Greedy Giant

by Lada Kratky

illustrated by Lane Yerkes

Read a Play

Genre

A **play** is a story that can be acted out. This play is about a family of farmers and a greedy giant.

Characters

Ana

Mamá

Papá

Giant

Seller

Neighbors

Setting

The play happens on a farm in Chile.

Chile

▲ farm in Chile

Selection Reading

1

Ana's family buys a farm. What is the big problem?

Narrator: One day, a farmer and his wife and their **clever** daughter Ana are walking in the country.

Seller: Hello, there. This nice field is for sale. Do you want to buy it?

Papá: We may buy it, if **the price is right**.

Seller: Oh, yes. The price is right. It is almost free!

Papá: Then we will buy it!

Neighbors: They will be sorry when the giant comes! Wait and see. Hee, hee, hee.

---

the price is right it doesn't cost too much money

Narrator: The family plows their new field. They stop when the greedy giant comes.

Giant: Wait! What do you think you are doing? This is my land! Here are my rules. You must give me part of what you **grow**.

Mamá: Why should we give you part of what we grow? We bought this field. Now it is ours!

Giant: I am the giant. I get what I want. And I want part of what you grow!

Ana: Which part do you want?

Giant: That's easy! I want the part that grows **above** the **ground** . You can keep what grows **below** the ground.

Ana: OK. **It's a deal**! Now go away, greedy Giant.

It's a deal We agree

Neighbors: They will be sorry when the giant comes back! Wait and see. Hee, hee, hee.

Papá: What will we do?

Ana: I have an idea. (whisper) Let's grow carrots!

Before You Move On

1. **Problem** What does the giant want? Why is this a problem?

2. **Inference** Why do the neighbors laugh?

2

Find out how Ana tries to solve the problem.

Narrator: So the family plows the **soil**, plants the seeds, and waters the field. The carrots grow and grow.

Mamá: It's **harvest time**!

Giant: And I am here to get my part.

Ana: Here is your part. The leaves are for you! The carrots grow below the ground, so we will keep them.

---

soil dirt

harvest time time to pick the vegetables

Giant: Grr! Next time, you keep what grows above the ground, and I keep what grows below.

Ana: OK. It's a deal!

Neighbors: They will be sorry when the giant comes back! Wait and see. Hee, hee, hee.

Ana: (whisper) Let's grow wheat!

Narrator: The family plows, plants, and waters the field. The wheat grows and grows.

Papá: It's harvest time again!

Giant: And I am here to get my part!

Ana: Here is your part. The roots are for you! The wheat grows above the ground, so we will keep it.

Giant: Not again! Next time, I keep what grows above *and* below the ground. You keep what grows **in between** .

Ana: It's a deal!

Neighbors: They will be sorry when the giant comes back! Wait and see. Hee, hee, hee.

Ana: (whisper) Let's grow corn!

Narrator: Again, the family plows the soil, plants the seeds, and waters the field. The corn grows and grows.

Mamá: It's harvest time again!

Giant: And I am here to get my part!

Ana: Here is your part, greedy Giant.
The roots and tassels are for you!
The ears of corn grow in between,
so we will keep them.

Giant: Oh, no! You
cheated me again.
That's not fair!

---

cheated me took the best part

Before You Move On

1. **Problem/Solution**
   What does Ana do to
   solve the problem?

2. **Inference** How do you
   think the giant feels?

93

3

What do you think the giant will do?

94

Papá: It's not fair? We plowed the soil!

Mamá: We planted the seeds!

Ana: We watered the field and gave
you the part you asked for!

Neighbors: They followed your rules.
We heard it all, and **fair is fair**.

Giant: Oh, **I give up**! You can keep
the field and everything you grow!

---

fair is fair they are right
I give up you win

Papá: The greedy giant is gone!

Mamá: Let's celebrate!

Ana: There is food for all,
so enjoy the **feast**!

All: Hurray!

---

feast party with
a lot of food

Before You Move On

1. **Inference** Why does
the giant leave?

2. **Character** Is Ana
clever? Why or
why not?

Meet the Playwright

Lada Kratky

Lada Kratky was born in Czechoslovakia. Her mother read folk tales to her when she was young. Her favorite tale was about a princess who was also named Lada!

Ms. Kratky likes folk tales because they can make her feel happy, sad, or scared. She loves to share stories with children around the world.

Think and Respond

Strategy: Problem and Solution

Some stories start with a problem. The story tells how a character solves the problem. Make a story map for "Clever Ana."

The **problem** starts the story.

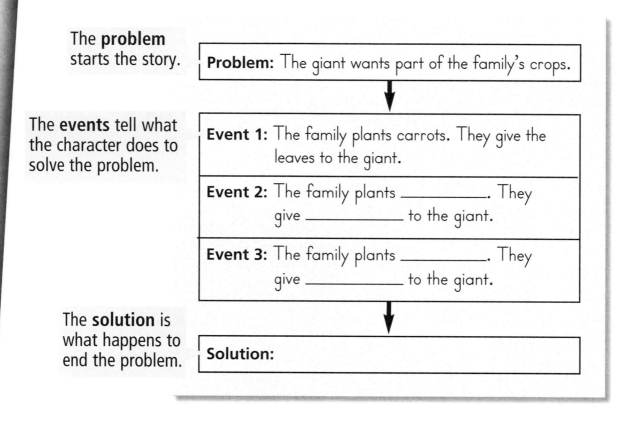

Problem: The giant wants part of the family's crops.

The **events** tell what the character does to solve the problem.

Event 1: The family plants carrots. They give the leaves to the giant.

Event 2: The family plants _____. They give _____ to the giant.

Event 3: The family plants _____. They give _____ to the giant.

The **solution** is what happens to end the problem.

Solution:

Real and Make-Believe

Look at your map. Which parts could happen in real life? Which parts are make-believe, or could not really happen?

Talk It Over

 Personal Response How are you like Ana? How are you different?

 Judgment Do you think the giant should get part of the crops? Why or why not?

3 **Personal Experience** Do you know someone who is clever like Ana? Explain.

Compare Stories

Compare Mrs. McNosh and "Clever Ana." What is real in each story? What is make-believe?

Content Connections

Listen to a Story

Listen to a story from Ecuador. Compare it to "Clever Ana and the Greedy Giant."

There is a giant in both stories.

large group

Experiment with Soil

Look at two kinds of soil. Which do you think is better for plants? Try an experiment to find out.

small group

100

Graph Plant Growth

Internet

1. Choose a vegetable.

2. Find out how long it takes to grow the vegetable from a seed.

3. Make a class bar graph of growing times.

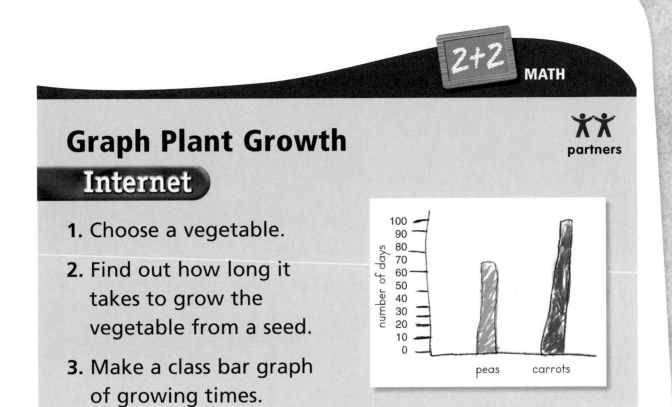

Write Dialogue

Look back at the art in the play. Write words for the mice to say.

Mouse 1: "The giant is mean!"

Mouse 2: "Yes, he is!"

Main Idea and Details

The **main idea** is the most important idea in a story. **Details** tell more about the main idea. To find the main idea and details:

✔ Think about the most important idea.
✔ Look for details that tell more about the main idea.

Try the strategy.

How Rice Grows

Rice needs different things to grow. Rice seeds are planted in fields filled with water. The roots of the rice plants get food from the water. Rice plants need sun, too. The rice grows in about three months.

The main idea is that rice needs different things to grow. "Rice plants need sun" is a detail.

Practice

Take this test and find the **main idea and details** .

Read thc article. Then read each question.
Mark the best answer.

Rice Is Nice

Many foods are made from rice. Breakfast cereal can be made from rice. Some desserts are made from rice, such as rice pudding. Even noodles can be made from rice flour.

1 What is the main idea for this diagram?

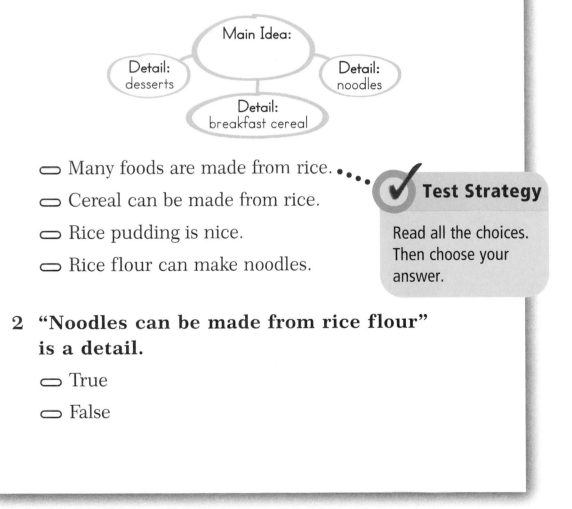

⬭ Many foods are made from rice.

⬭ Cereal can be made from rice.

⬭ Rice pudding is nice.

⬭ Rice flour can make noodles.

> ✓ **Test Strategy**
>
> Read all the choices. Then choose your answer.

2 "Noodles can be made from rice flour" is a detail.

⬭ True

⬭ False

Family Farming

Grandpa tells me about **dairy farming** long ago. He took care of cows.

Grandpa milks his cow.

small market

Grandpa made dairy **products** to sell at a small **market** .

vegetable farm where Dad works

Key Words

dairy

farming

product

market

vegetable

factory

machine

My dad is a farmer today. He works on a big **vegetable** farm. The farm sends the vegetables to a **factory**. **Machines** get the food ready to go to stores.

factory

Read Social Studies

A **nonfiction article** gives facts about a topic.

- ✔ Look for **headings**. They tell you what the sections are about.
- ✔ Read the **captions** under the photos to learn more.

heading → 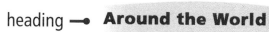 **Around the World**

Farming is important all around the world. Different crops grow in different parts of the world.

Arctic Ocean

NORTH
AMERICA

Pacific
Ocean

Atla
Oce

SOUTH
AMERIC

caption → ▲ Artichokes grow in California.

Selection Reading

Farms

by Sylvia Madrigal

Take a seed. No, take thousands of seeds.
Plant them all in the ground, in row after row.

row

Add a few special **machines** and some very important workers. Be sure there is enough water and sun. Do you know what you have made?

▲ tractor and driver

▲ field workers

harvester

Vegetable Farm

A **vegetable** farm!

Farming is the most important activity in the world. People cannot live without food. Almost all the food we eat is grown on farms.

There are many other kinds of farms that **produce** food.

_____

produce grow

▲ broccoli farm

▲ lettuce farm

Before You Move On

1. **Cause/Effect** Why is farming important?
2. **Details** What kind of vegetables grow on vegetable farms?

Dairy Farm

A **dairy** farm has cows, cows, and more cows! Did you know that the milk you drink comes from milk cows like these?

▼ Cows eat grass.

▲ Sometimes cows eat silage.

Cows have to eat to make milk. When the **pastures** are green, cows eat grass. When the grass is brown during the fall and winter, they eat hay or silage. Hay is dry grass. Silage is food made from **dried corn stalks**.

---

pastures fields

dried corn stalks corn stems that are dry, or not green anymore

Before You Move On

1. **Cause/Effect** What do cows have to do to make milk?

2. **Conclusion** Why do cows eat hay in the winter?

113

From Cow to Market

tank

truck

MILK

1 Machines milk the cows.

2 The milk goes to a tank. A truck takes the milk to a dairy.

Dairy farmers **milk the cows** two times each day.
In the past, people milked the cows by hand.
Today farmers use milking machines to do the job.

_____

milk the cows get milk from cows

114

3 The dairy makes **products** like butter, yogurt, cheese, and milk.

4 Another truck takes the products to the **market** .

Before You Move On

1. **Graphic Aids** How does milk go from cow to market?

2. **Comparison** How did farmers milk cows in the past? Today?

115

Wheat Farm

This is a field of **ripe wheat**. It is huge. You can see golden stalks of wheat for miles and miles. Some people think wheat is the most important food in the world.

_____

ripe wheat wheat that is finished growing

bread

flour tortillas

cereal

noodles

Think of the many foods made from wheat: bread, flour tortillas, cereals, and noodles.

You probably eat something made from wheat every day.

Before You Move On

1. **Conclusion** Why is wheat important?
2. **Details** Name three foods made from wheat.

117

From Field to Factory

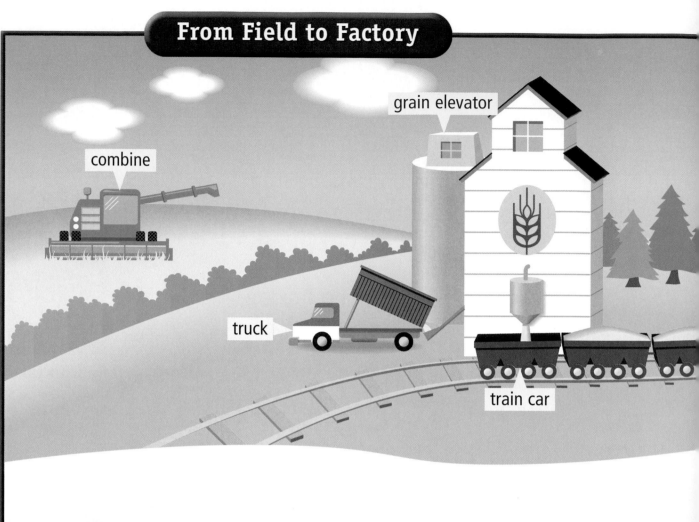

1 A combine harvests the wheat from the field.

2 A truck takes the wheat to a tank called a grain elevator.

railroad tracks

mill

CEREAL

Flour

3 The wheat grain goes into a train car. The train takes the wheat to a **factory** called a mill.

4 The mill grinds the wheat to make flour and other products.

Before You Move On

1. **Details** What happens at the mill?

2. **Sequence** How does grain go from the field to the factory?

Orange Farm

Orange farmers do not have to plant their crop every year. Orange trees grow and produce oranges for many years.

Orange farmers also do not need many machines to harvest the fruit. Workers pick the oranges from the trees. They use ladders to reach the oranges high up in the trees.

ladder

U.S. Orange-Growing States

California

Arizona

Texas

Florida

■ States that grow the most oranges

Oranges and other citrus fruit grow in places that are warm. California, Arizona, Texas, and Florida are warm almost all year long. These states produce most of the oranges in the U.S.

Before You Move On

1. **Comparison** How is an orange farm different from a wheat farm?

2. **Graphic Aids** Which states produce the most oranges?

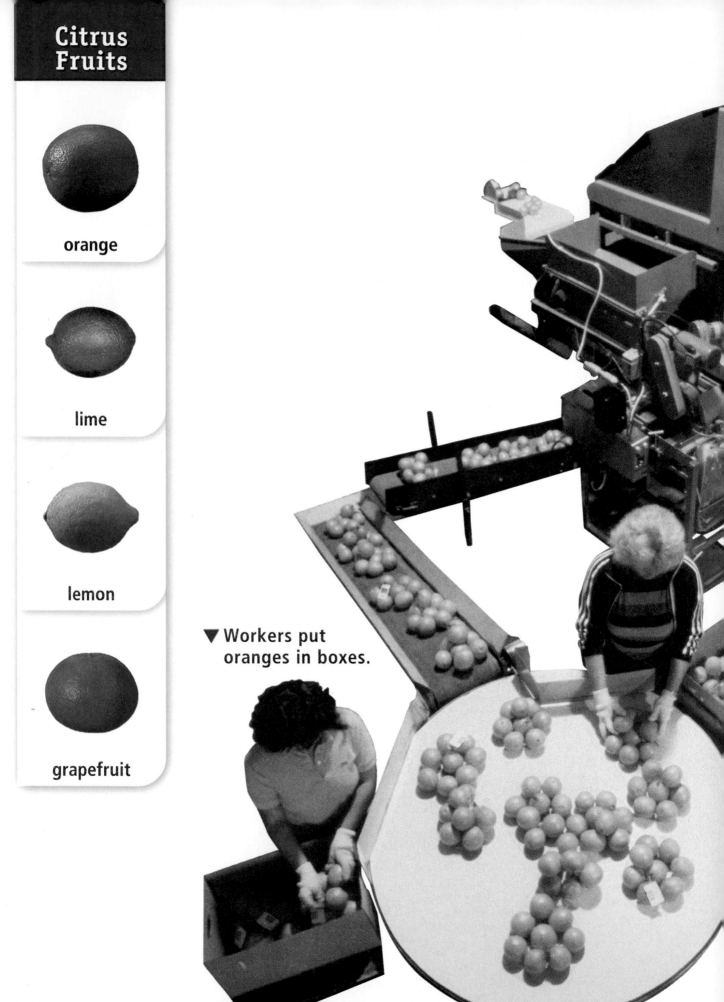

Citrus Fruits

orange

lime

lemon

grapefruit

▼ Workers put oranges in boxes.

Some oranges go to markets after they are picked. First, trucks take them to a building. The oranges are sorted by size. People put them into boxes. Then trucks take the boxes of oranges to markets around the country.

Other oranges go to factories. At the factory, people check each orange to make sure it is good. Then they make orange juice and other products.

Before You Move On

1. **Sequence** What happens after the fruit is picked?

2. **Judgment** Do you think farming is hard work? Why or why not?

Around the World

Farming is important all around the world. Different crops grow in different parts of the world.

▲ Artichokes grow in California.

▲ Bananas grow in Brazil.

▲ Tea grows in Kenya.

Farms give us many things: vegetables, milk, grain, and fruit. Farms send their products to market. Then products go from the market to you!

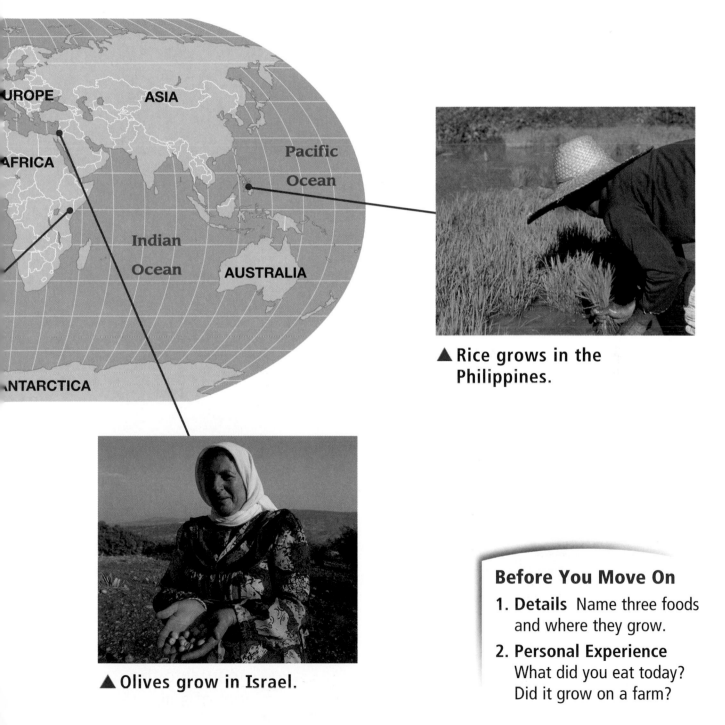

▲ Rice grows in the Philippines.

▲ Olives grow in Israel.

Before You Move On

1. **Details** Name three foods and where they grow.

2. **Personal Experience** What did you eat today? Did it grow on a farm?

125

HOW TO GROW CORN

You will need:

a sponge

a clear plastic cup

four kernels of field corn

a five-gallon pot of soil

water

Grow corn in your classroom! Here's how:

1 Push the sponge into the cup.

2 Put the kernels between the sponge and the cup.

3 Pour an inch of water into the cup.

4 Put the cup in a sunny place. Water it when it gets dry.

5 Wait until the sprouts pop out.

6 When the sprouts are three to four inches tall, put them into the pot of soil.

It should take about twelve weeks for your kernel to grow into a corn plant.

- Watch what happens as the sprout grows into corn. Take notes.

- When the stalk is two feet tall, plant it outside.

- The corn needs to be seven to eight feet tall to make an ear of corn.

tassel

stalk

leaf

husk

ear of corn

Before You Move On

1. **Steps in a Process** What do you do after Step 1?

2. **Details** What will help the corn plant grow?

Think and Respond

Strategy: Main Idea and Details

A main idea is what a story is mostly about. Details tell about the main idea. Make a main idea diagram for "Farms."

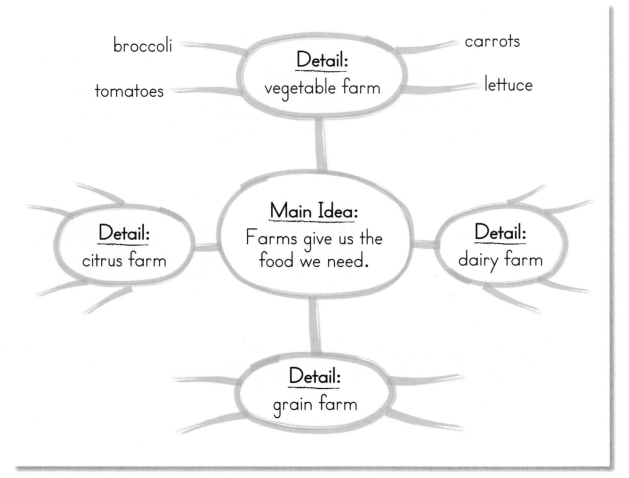

broccoli

tomatoes

Detail: vegetable farm

carrots

lettuce

Detail: citrus farm

Main Idea: Farms give us the food we need.

Detail: dairy farm

Detail: grain farm

Plan a Meal

Use your completed diagram to plan a meal. Include one food product from each farm in your menu. Compare your menu to a partner's menu.

Talk It Over

1 **Personal Response** What is your favorite food from the article? Where does it grow?

2 **Conclusion** Can people live without farms? Why or why not?

3 **Generalization** How are all farms the same?

Compare Topics

Compare what you learned about farming in "Clever Ana and the Greedy Giant" with what you learned in "Farms."

I learned some farms are small like Ana's. Some are big and use machines.

Content Connections

ART

Make a Corn Product

partners

Make a product from corn. Decide what price to put on your product. "Sell" your product in a classroom market.

SOCIAL STUDIES

Make a Product Map

Internet

partners

Choose a country. Research what crops grow there. Put symbols of the crops on a world map, and tell your class about them.

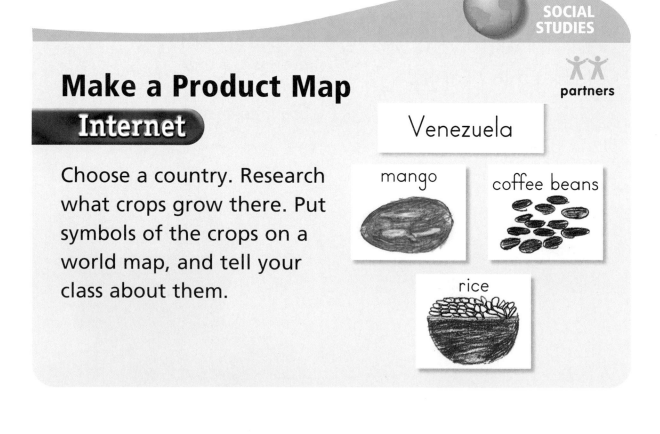

Venezuela

mango

coffee beans

rice

Interview a Farmer

The farmer grows cabbage.

large group

Invite a farmer or a gardener to your class. Make a list of questions you want to ask. Take notes as you listen to the answers. What did you learn? What else do you want to know?

WRITING

Write Directions

on your own

Write directions for making your favorite sandwich. What do you need? What do you do first?

You Will Need:
turkey
cheese
mustard
two pieces of bread

1. Put the bread on a plate.
2. Spread mustard on one piece of bread.

Action Verbs

Listen and sing.

Song 🔘

The Farmers' Market

Mama shops on Saturday.

She looks at the vegetables

On display.

She talks to farmers

While they weigh

Bags of vegetables.

Then she pays.

—Joyce McGreevy

25¢ each

40¢ each

35¢ each

20¢ each

$1 00

50¢ each

Tune: "Jack, Be Nimble"

How Language Works

An **action verb** tells what someone or something does. To tell about one other person or thing, add –**s** to the verb.

She	He	It
Mama shop**s**.	He sell**s** corn.	It taste**s** good.

Practice with a Partner

Choose the correct red verb. Then say each sentence.

plant / plants   **1.** The farmer _____ seeds in the soil.

grow / grows   **2.** The seeds _____ into plants.

shine / shines   **3.** The sun _____ on the plants.

water / waters   **4.** The children _____ the plants.

Put It in Writing!

Write a sentence about something that happens in a garden. When you edit your work, make sure your verbs are correct.

Mom pulls weeds.

Show What You Know

Talk About Farms and Food

Look back at the unit. What is the most interesting thing you learned? Share your ideas with a group.

Make a Mind Map

Show what you learned about food.

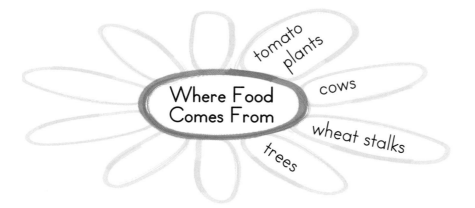

Think and Write

What questions do you still have about farms or food? Make a list. Add the list to your portfolio.

Read and Learn More

Leveled Books

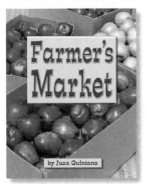

Farmer's Market
by Juan Quintana

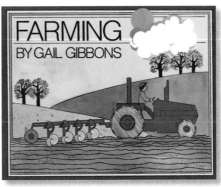

Farming
by Gail Gibbons

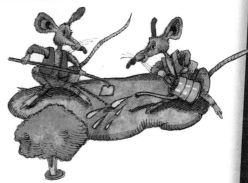

Theme Library

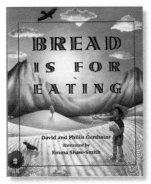

Bread Is for Eating
by David and Phillis Gershator

Molly and Emmett's Surprise Garden
by Marylin Hafner

Internet

Go to: www.hbavenues.com

Grow Food

Farm Life

All About Cows

Water, Water, Everywhere

Do a Water Cycle Experiment

1. Make a cloud.
2. Watch what happens in the jar.
3. Talk about what you see.

Science Words

Land and Water

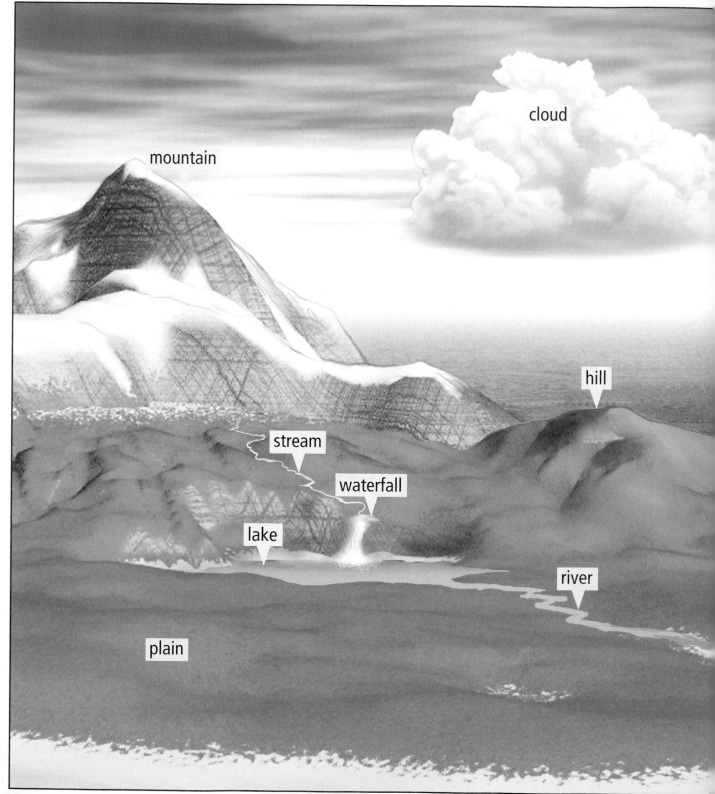

cloud

mountain

hill

stream

waterfall

lake

river

plain

Song

Puddles to the Sky

Puddles are made when

The rainwater **flows**.

Sun comes out.

Rain **clouds** go.

Water drops **rise**

And then they **disappear**,

In the sky,

Tell me why.

—Joyce McGreevy

Tune: "The Windmill"

Key Words

puddle

flow

cloud

water

rise

disappear

Read a Science Article

A **science article** is nonfiction. It tells how and why something happens.

✔ Look for **diagrams**. Diagrams can show how something works.

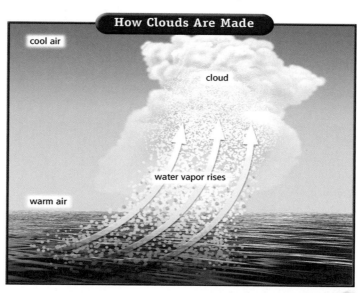

How Clouds Are Made

cool air

cloud

water vapor rises

warm air

Selection Reading

Where Do Puddles Go?

by Fay Robinson

▲ **Rain makes the path wet.**

Do you like to watch the rain **pour** down from the sky, soaking trees and plants and streets and sidewalks? Then, right after it rains, do you ever put on your boots and jump in the **puddles**?

---

pour come, fall

▲ **The sun dries the path.**

When the sun comes out, everything **dries up**, and the puddles **disappear** . Where do they go?

_____

dries up gets dry

Before You Move On

1. **Cause/Effect** Where do puddles come from?
2. **Inference** Why do puddles disappear?

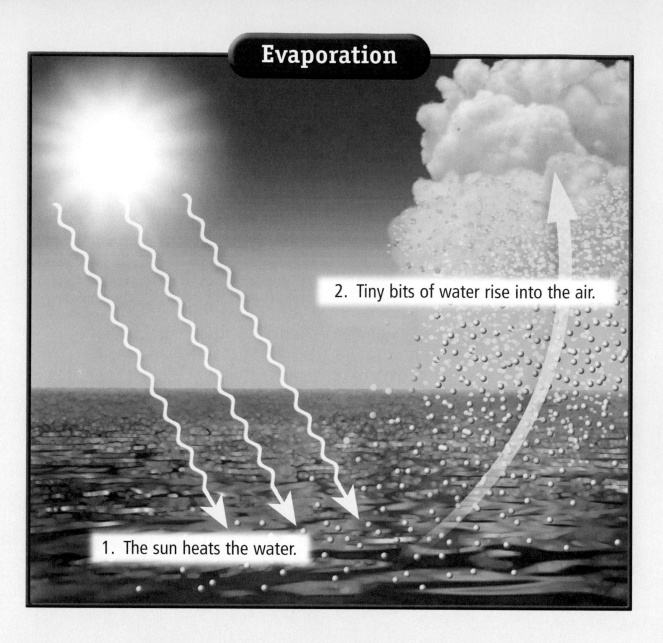

Evaporation

2. Tiny bits of water rise into the air.

1. The sun heats the water.

Puddles dry up because of the sun. Heat from the sun warms the smallest parts of each drop of **water** .

Warm air **rises** , and the **tiny** bits of water rise, too. They become part of the air. This is called evaporation.

---

tiny very small

Where Does the Water Go?

▲ first day   ▲ after 1 day   ▲ after 2 days

Water that has evaporated is called water vapor.
Water vapor is invisible—you can't see it.

Before You Move On

1. **Graphic Aids** What happens when water evaporates?

2. **Details** Can you see water vapor?

How Clouds Are Made

cool air

cloud

water vapor rises

warm air

Water vapor rises high into the sky. The air is cooler up there. The cool air makes the tiny drops of water in vapor **join together**. Soon there are so many drops in one place that you can see them. That's what **clouds** are.

---

join together become one thing

148

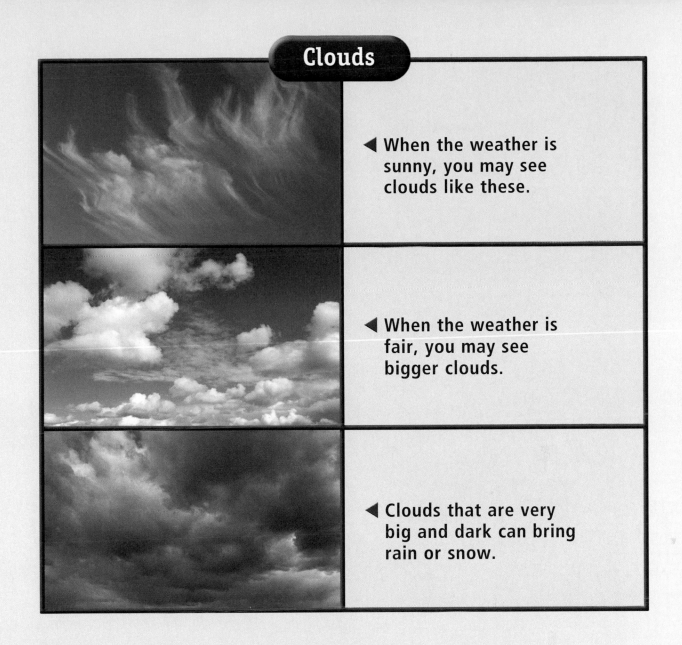

Clouds

◀ When the weather is sunny, you may see clouds like these.

◀ When the weather is fair, you may see bigger clouds.

◀ Clouds that are very big and dark can bring rain or snow.

There are different kinds of clouds. Some are big and puffy and white.

Some are so full of water that they turn gray. Then, **heavy** drops of water fall to the ground as rain. If it is cold enough outside, it snows instead.

---

heavy big

Before You Move On

1. **Cause/Effect** What does cool air do to water vapor?
2. **Conclusion** What is inside a cloud?

149

Rainwater doesn't always evaporate right away.
A lot of it trickles into **streams** and rivers.

_____

streams small rivers

The streams and rivers **flow** into lakes and oceans.

Before You Move On

1. **Details** What happens when rainwater does not evaporate right away?

2. **Viewing** What does this photo show you?

151

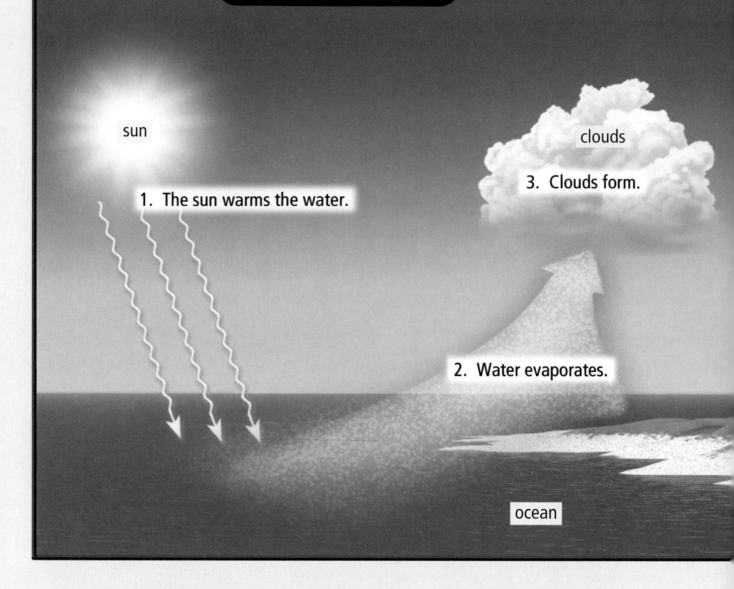

The Water Cycle

sun

1. The sun warms the water.

clouds

3. Clouds form.

2. Water evaporates.

ocean

The sun heats up the lakes and oceans like giant puddles. Water on the **surface** evaporates and rises into the sky.

It **collects as** clouds and falls as rain again. This pattern is called the water cycle.

---

surface top
collects as makes

4. Water falls as rain.

rain

lake

river

The water cycle never stops. All the water we have on Earth is all we ever had. From **prehistoric times** until now, the same water is used over and over again.

---

prehistoric times long, long ago

Before You Move On

1. **Details** What does the sun do to water?
2. **Graphic Aids** What is a cycle?

▲ mountain snowstorm

▲ waterfall

▲ A killer whale spouts water.

The water you use today may someday fall in a mountain snowstorm, **crash** over a cliff in a waterfall, or **spout from** a whale in an ocean.

———————————

crash drop quickly
spout from come out of

Or it may **fill** a puddle you jump
in right after it rains.

---

fill go into

Before You Move On

1. **Comparison** How are
   these photos the same?

2. **Paraphrase** Name three
   places water might go
   after you use it today.

Think and Respond

Strategy: Sequence

The sequence shows things in order. Add the missing steps to the water cycle.

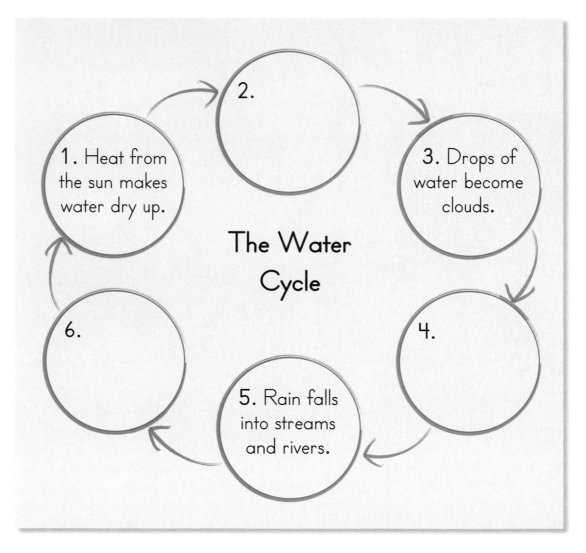

The Water Cycle

1. Heat from the sun makes water dry up.

2.

3. Drops of water become clouds.

4.

5. Rain falls into streams and rivers.

6.

Explain

Use your diagram to tell how the water cycle works.

Talk It Over

 Personal Response What did you learn about water from the article?

 Steps in a Process Imagine that you are a drop of water in a puddle. Tell how you become a cloud.

3 **Conclusion** Do we drink the same water today that dinosaurs drank long ago? Why or why not?

Compare Nonfiction

Compare "Where Do Puddles Go?" and "Farms." How are they alike? How are they different?

Both articles have diagrams to show how things work.

Content Connections

Give a Weather Report
Internet

Listen to a weather report.
Then tell your class what
the weather will be like.

Today, it
will rain.

small group

2+2   MATH

Make a Graph

large group

1. Make a list of three people
   you know.

2. Ask each person, "What
   is your favorite kind
   of weather?"

3. Use the answers to make a
   class bar graph.

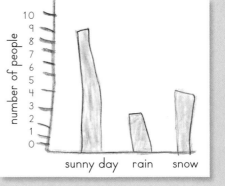

Be a Water Detective

partners

Watch how people use water for one week. Write what you see. Research how people can save water. Make a poster to show how to save water.

Turn off the faucet.

Write a Story

on your own

Write a story about a drop of water. What does it do? Where does it go? What does it see?

Today, Danny the Drop disappeared. Yesterday, he was in a puddle. Today, the puddle is gone.

Make Predictions

When you guess what will happen next in a story, you **make a prediction** . To make predictions:

✔ Look for story clues.
✔ Think about what you already know.

Try the strategy.

Rain Gear

Tia gets her raincoat and boots out of the closet. She needs her rain hat, too. She puts on the raincoat, boots, and hat. Then she walks out the door.

> The story says that Tia puts on a raincoat, boots, and a hat. I wear those things when it rains. I predict that Tia will go outside in the rain.

Practice

Take this test and make predictions .

Read the rest of the story. Then read each question. Mark the best answer.

Tia goes outside.
"I'm ready!" she says.
The sun is shining on her father's car. Her father is holding a hose and a pail of soapy water. He smiles when he sees Tia in her rain clothes. He gives her a sponge.

1 **What do you think will happen next?**

○ Tia will cry.

○ Tia's father will walk the dog.

○ Tia and her father will wash the car.

○ Tia and her father will drive to the store.

2 **Which clue helps you make the prediction?**

○ Tia's father gives her a sponge.

○ Tia's father smiles when he sees her.

○ Tia goes outside.

○ Tia likes the sun.

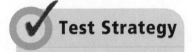

Test Strategy

Do you know the answer? If you don't, read the story again.

A Plant Problem

Dear Plant Doctor:

I am **afraid** I cannot **save** my plant! It **became** **dry**. Should I give it to a **friend**?

Thanks,
Jannah

Key Words

afraid

save

became

friend

give away

idea

Dear Jannah:

Don't give away your plant yet! I have an idea to help you. Try to water it once a week.

**Good luck,
The Plant Doctor**

Eva's Cloud

by Bertrand Ruillé
English version by Guadalupe López
illustrated by Enrique O. Sánchez

Read a Story

Genre

A **fantasy** is make-believe. It tells a story that cannot really happen. This fantasy is about a girl and a cloud.

Characters

Eva

Cloud

Setting

The story happens in the country during a time when there is no rain.

▲ countryside with no rain

Selection Reading

1

Once upon a time, a girl named Eva
lived in the country. One summer morning,
Eva was playing outside. She looked up and
saw a special cloud.

"Come and play with me!" called Eva.
The cloud smiled. It **floated** down to Eva.

_____
floated moved slowly

166

"Good morning, Eva," said the cloud.
"Good morning, Cloud!" answered Eva.
Eva and the cloud soon became **friends**.
Every morning, the cloud would wake Eva.
They would play together all day. Then the
cloud would say good night and float away
until the next morning.

Eva loved to hide in the cloud. Inside, everything was white and smelled wonderful. The cloud smelled like flowers and grass after it slept in the field. The cloud smelled like pine trees after it slept in the forest.

Some days, Eva would take cloud baths.
When she stepped out of the cloud, her skin
was **moist** and fresh.

But Eva could not stay in
the cloud for very long. It was
a little hard to breathe in there.

―――――――――
moist a little wet

Before You Move On

1. **Details** What happens
   when the cloud sleeps
   in the field?

2. **Inference** Why is Eva's
   skin moist?

The cloud is sad. Read to find out why.

The days passed, and the summer **became** hot and dry. There was no rain for a long, long time.

The leaves and grass turned brown. The flowers became sad and **wilted**. The animals could not find water to drink.

─────────────

wilted hanging down

170

Lorenzo, the big sheep, **suffered the most** because he had a lot of **wool**. Lorenzo had more wool than any other sheep in the country. All that wool made Lorenzo very hot.

---

suffered the most felt the worst
wool hair

Even Grace, the butterfly, could not find
a drop of water to drink in the flowers.
Poor Grace had lost all her colors.

The cloud was very sad. It was **afraid**
that the plants and the animals would die.

So early one morning, while Eva was still asleep, the cloud said to itself, "I'm going to **save** them."

The cloud began to cry. It moved along from place to place very slowly, watering everything with its tears.

Before You Move On
1. **Cause/Effect** Why does Grace lose her colors?
2. **Conclusion** Is rain important? Why?

The grass turned green again. The
animals drank and drank from the pond.
But as the cloud **gave away** more
and more of its water, it grew smaller
and smaller.

174

By the time it reached Lorenzo, the
cloud was no bigger than the sheep. But
the cloud rained on Lorenzo for a while.
Lorenzo was so happy to have a
cool shower!

By the time the cloud reached Grace,
it was no bigger than she was.

"If I give away any more water," thought
the cloud, "I will surely disappear."

But still, the cloud gave a little water
to Grace. Grace drank until the colors
returned to her wings.

---

returned to came back into

By this time, Eva was awake.

"I wonder why the cloud did not come to wake me up this morning," said Eva.

Eva looked out her window and saw green fields. Ah! Now she knew what had happened.

Eva ran outside.

By this time Now

Before You Move On

1. **Cause/Effect** Why does the cloud get smaller?
2. **Character** Do you think the cloud is nice? Why or why not?

177

4

Find out what Eva does to help the cloud.

"Where are you, Cloud?" Eva called out. The cloud had given so much water that it was almost gone. Still, it heard Eva's voice. The cloud used all its strength to lift itself into the air. How tiny it was! But Eva saw it.

Eva carried the cloud home and into the kitchen. On the table, there was a cup of steaming hot chocolate.

"Hurry," said the cloud. "Put me over the cup!" Eva did, and the cloud began to drink the **vapor**.

All day long, Eva brought steaming cups to the cloud. By night, the cloud was a little fatter. But it was still very tiny.

---

vapor water drops

Then Eva had an **idea**. She ran outside and shouted:

"Listen, my animal friends! Tomorrow morning, when the air is cool and **damp**, I want everyone to gather together so we can save the cloud."

"Yes! Yes!" answered all the animals.

---

damp wet

The next morning, all of the animals
came to save the cloud. Even the snails and
the worms came. They blew and blew into
the cool morning air, and their breath
turned to vapor.

The cloud drank the vapor and grew
bigger and bigger.

Lorenzo blew as hard as he could.
He really wanted to save the cloud!

Grace wanted to help, too. But she had
a cold and she couldn't breathe well. Still,
she did what she could.

"I feel a little better. Thank you, Eva.
Thank you, animals," said the cloud.

"I'm glad you are feeling better, Cloud,"
answered Eva. "But you are still too small.
You must go to the ocean and to the
mountains. The **mist and the fog** will
make you healthy again."

_____

mist and the fog wet air

"You're right," said the cloud. "I should go. I promise that I will return."

Eva and the animals waved goodbye as the cloud floated away to the ocean.

The cloud <u>will</u> return. You can be sure of that.

Before You Move On

1. **Cause/Effect** What helps the cloud?

2. **Predict** What will happen to the cloud at the ocean?

Meet the Illustrator

Enrique O. Sánchez

Enrique O. Sánchez is from the Dominican Republic. He moved to the United States to become an artist. At his first job, he helped the artists who worked for the children's TV show "Sesame Street."

Mr. Sánchez now lives on a mountain in Vermont. For fun, he paints country settings. He likes "to see and paint the colors of nature."

Think and Respond

Strategy: Identify Plot

In most stories, things happen in a certain order. These events are the story's plot. Make a story map for "Eva's Cloud."

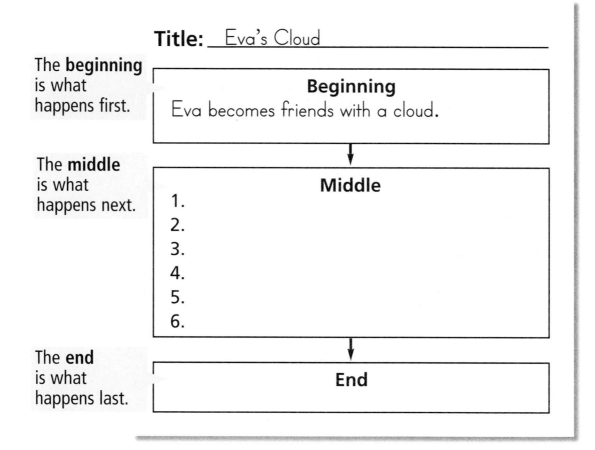

Title: Eva's Cloud

The **beginning** is what happens first.

Beginning
Eva becomes friends with a cloud.

The **middle** is what happens next.

Middle
1.
2.
3.
4.
5.
6.

The **end** is what happens last.

End

Retell the Story

Choose one event. Stand with your friends in the order of the plot. Each person retells his or her event in the story.

Talk It Over

 Personal Response Do you like the story? What is your favorite part?

 Summarize How does the cloud help the animals? How does Eva help the cloud?

3 **Inference** Do you think Eva is sad in the end when the cloud goes away? Why or why not?

Compare Themes

Compare "Eva's Cloud" to other friendship stories you know.

Content Connections

Add to the Story

What happens to the cloud after it leaves Eva? Talk about your ideas with your group. Tell your new story to the class.

The cloud gets big again at the ocean.

small group

Read a Map
Internet

partners

Eva's cloud must go to mountains and oceans to get bigger. Look at a map in a book or on the Internet. Find out where Eva's cloud could find mountains and oceans.

Canada

United States of America

Pacific Ocean

Atlantic Ocean

Gulf of Mexico

Mexico

N W E S

Compare Rainfall

small group

Look in books to find out how much rain falls in a U.S. city. Add your data to a class table. Compare rainfall in the United States.

Town	Rainfall
Denver	15 inches
Our Town	16 inches
Orlando	48 inches

WRITING

Write a Thank-You Note

on your own

Pretend you are one of the animals in "Eva's Cloud." How did the cloud help you? Write a thank-you note to the cloud.

November 15

Dear Cloud,
    Thank you for giving me a shower. I really needed it!

Adjectives

Listen and sing.

Song

Dark Clouds

Dark clouds bring snow and rain

Until the sunny skies return.

Soon skies are blue again

And I run out to play.

—Joyce McGreevy

Tune: "Early One Morning"

How Language Works

Adjectives	Examples
■ Adjectives tell what something is like.	I see **big** clouds. The sky is **gray**.
■ Adjectives tell how many.	I feel **three** raindrops.

Practice with a Partner

Put the red word where it goes in the sentence.
Then say the sentence.

dark **1.** Luz looks at the sky.

two **2.** She sees snowflakes on her hand.

cold **3.** She feels a wind.

warm **4.** She goes into her house.

Put It in Writing!

Write about a rainy day.
Tell what it is like.

The wind is strong.

Show What You Know

Talk About the Water Cycle

Look back at the selections and find your favorite passage. Read it aloud to your group. Tell why it is your favorite.

Water Words

On a separate piece of paper, write the names of different forms of water in the raindrops.

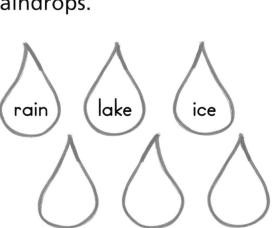

rain   lake   ice

Think and Write

Write about how you use water every day. Add this writing to your portfolio.

Read and Learn More

Leveled Books

Water
by Frank Asch

The Little Ant
by Shirleyann Costigan

Theme Library

Storm Is Coming!
by Heather Tekavec

This Is the Rain
by Lola M. Schaefer

Internet

Go to: www.hbavenues.com

Follow the Rain Drop

Geography

Cloud Games

Celebrate!

Role-Play a Celebration

1. Talk about a celebration.
2. Pretend you are at that celebration.
3. Act out what you do and say.

Celebrations

Some holidays are celebrated in many countries.
Some are celebrated in only one country.

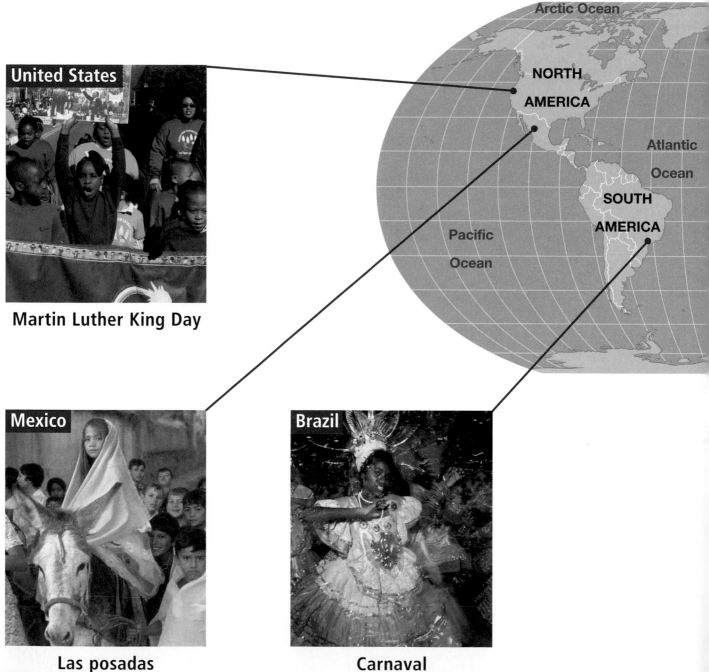

United States

Martin Luther King Day

Mexico

Las posadas

Brazil

Carnaval

Arctic Ocean

NORTH AMERICA

Atlantic Ocean

SOUTH AMERICA

Pacific Ocean

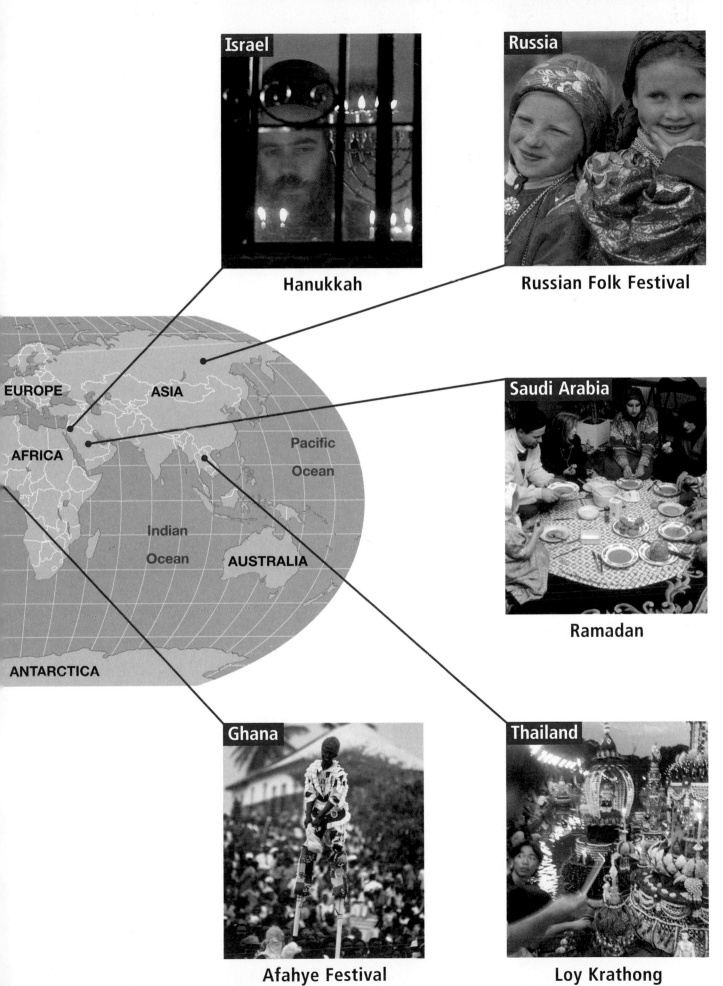

Israel

Hanukkah

Russia

Russian Folk Festival

Saudi Arabia

Ramadan

Ghana

Afahye Festival

Thailand

Loy Krathong

EUROPE

ASIA

AFRICA

Pacific Ocean

Indian Ocean

AUSTRALIA

ANTARCTICA

A Letter to Grandma

trumpet practice

July 3

Dear Grandma,

Tomorrow is the town parade. I will march and play the trumpet. I am scared because I have **trouble** marching and playing at the same time.

parade

Key Words

trouble

neighbor

brave

dream

luck

envelope

The **neighbors** next door will be there with Mom. I will try to be strong and **brave**. My **dream** is to play well. Wish me **luck**!

Love,
Bridgit

envelope

Grandma
123 Main Street
San Antonio, TX 78230

This Next New Year

by Janet S. Wong • illustrated by Yangsook Choi

Read a Story

Genre

This story tells about events that could really happen. It is **realistic fiction** . In the story, a boy tells how his family prepares for a New Year's celebration.

Characters

boy

family

friends

Setting

This story happens during Chinese New Year.

▲ a Chinese New Year parade

Selection Reading

Find out how the boy celebrates Chinese New Year.

This next new year **is about to begin**,

not the regular new year, January 1,

when we watch the Rose Parade and football games

---

is about to begin will start soon

and make **crazy
New Year's resolutions**,

but the lunar new year,
the day of the first new moon.

---

crazy New Year's resolutions
promises that are too hard to keep

I call it Chinese New Year
even though I **am half Korean**

and my mother cooks *duk gook*,
the Korean new year soup.

---

am half Korean have one parent
who is Korean

My best friend Glenn, who is French and German,
calls it Chinese New Year, too,

even though he celebrates it at his house
by eating **Thai food to go**.

Thai food to go food from a Thai
restaurant that he takes home

And my other best friend Evelyn,
who **is part Hopi and part Mexican**,

says Chinese New Year
is her favorite holiday

because she likes to get red **envelopes** **stuffed with**
money from her **neighbor** who came from Singapore.

---

is part Hopi and part Mexican has one
Hopi parent and one Mexican parent
stuffed with full of

This next new year
is going to be good,

the best year ever.
I can feel it in my hands.

They say you are **coming into** money
when your palms itch,

and my palms have been itching
for days.

My brother thinks it's **warts**,
but I know the luck is coming

because we've started early, for once,
and our luck **is long overdue**.

They Some people
coming into getting
warts small bumps
is long overdue should have
come long ago

Before You Move On

1. **Details** How do people celebrate this holiday?
2. **Inference** Do only Chinese people celebrate Chinese New Year? How do you know?

The boy
cleans the
house and
himself.
Find out
why.

Mother is sweeping last year's **dust**
into piles so big

all I can figure is
no wonder we've had so much  **trouble** lately.

---

dust dirt
all I can figure is no wonder I guess
that is why

I will move these mountains of bad luck
off the floor and into the trash,

brushing every last **crummy crumb**
into my dustpan.

_____

crummy crumb piece of dirt

One last piece of the porcelain vase
that broke when the ball

slipped out of my hand—
gone!

A river of leaves from the plant
that died even though I **meant**

to water it soon—
gone!

A river of Many
meant wanted

The cricket I found one day in my shoe
who made a good pet

until he **escaped**—
Oh, poor cricket, I looked for you—

all that bad luck,
gone!

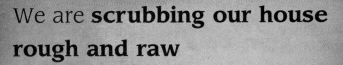

We are **scrubbing our house
rough and raw**

so it can **soak up** good luck
like an empty sponge.

---

escaped ran away

scrubbing our house rough and raw
cleaning our house well

soak up pull in

And tonight I am washing my hair
and drying it extra dry

so it can soak up some good luck, too,
and that luck can drip into my brain

and **come to my rescue**
at school.

---

come to my rescue help me

I am cutting my nails
and even cleaning the dirt out from the corners

of my big toenails
so the luck can **squeeze itself in there**

and take me
where I want to go.

———————

squeeze itself in there get inside

I am flossing my teeth
so I will have something smart to say

next time
you **catch me by surprise**.

_____

catch me by surprise surprise me

Before You Move On

1. **Character** What mistakes does the boy make during the year?

2. **Details** What does the boy do to get luck?

3

What will
the boy
do on the
big day?

I don't have the new clothes I need
but I have saved the cleanest ones I own

for this big day
and if **everything works**

you can bet
I will have new clothes soon.

_____

everything works good luck comes

This year I am not going to **jump out of my skin**
when we light the firecrackers at midnight

to scare the bad luck away
and wake up all the neighbors.

I will be brave .

---

jump out of my skin be scared

I will not even hide my face
inside the **crowd** during the parade

_____

crowd large group of people

when they light the long strings of firecrackers
that pop pop pop pop pop pop pop

all over the place.

And all day tomorrow,
Lunar New Year's Day,

I will not say one **awful** thing,
none of that

> *can't do*
> *don't have*
> *why me*

because this is it, a **fresh start**,
my second chance,

---

awful bad
fresh start new beginning

and I have so many **dreams** ,
so many dreams

I'm ready
now

to make
come true.

Before You Move On

1. **Character** What did the boy do last year during this holiday?

2. **Inference** What is a fresh start?

Meet the Author

Janet S. Wong

AWARD WINNER

Janet Wong is half Korean and half Chinese, like the boy in "This Next New Year." Most of Ms. Wong's stories are about growing up in more than one culture.

"This Next New Year" is a story, but it is also a long poem. Ms. Wong likes poetry because it gives her a strong feeling. "Poetry is like shouting," she says.

Rosh Ha-Shanah Eve

Stale moon, climb down.
Clear the sky.
Get out of town.
Good-bye.

Fresh moon, arise.
Throw a glow.
Shine a surprise.
Hello.

New Year, amen.
Now we begin:
Teach me to be a new me.

—Harry Philip

Before You Move On

Comparison How is Rosh Ha-Shanah like the Chinese New Year?

231

Kwanzaa Is...

One day after Christmas comes,
we listen to the Kwanzaa drums
and celebrate for seven days
our old customs and modern ways.

—Cedric McClester

Mawlid Al-Nabi

Mawlid is a very happy day.
We dress up the house
With the names of the Prophet.
We eat special food,
We pray
And we remember.
We light candles
And light up the night.
We sing the praises
Of the Prophet Muhammad
Because it's his birthday.

—Karam Sperling

Before You Move On

Details What do people do for Kwanzaa and Mawlid Al-Nabi?

Think and Respond

Strategy: Analyze Character

Characters are the people in a story. Make a chart to show how the boy prepares for the lunar new year. Look for:

- ✔ what the boy does
- ✔ why the boy does it.

What does the boy do?	Why does the boy do it?
He eats duk gook soup.	It's the Korean New Year soup.

Interview the Character

Pretend you are a newspaper reporter. Your partner can play the boy. Interview him about how and why he prepares for the lunar new year.

Talk It Over

1 **Personal Response** The boy does many things to prepare for the new year. What do you do?

2 **Comparison** How is January 1 different than the lunar new year?

3 **Opinion** Do you think it is important to have a fresh start? Why or why not?

Compare Ideas

Compare what you learned about holidays in "This Next New Year" with what you learned from the poems.

Content Connections

Celebration Scenes

Act out part of a celebration from the story or one of the poems. Talk about how the celebrations are alike and different.

Chinese New Year and Mawlid Al-Nabi both have special food.

Make a Calendar

Internet

Choose a year in the future. Find out when the first new Moon of that year will be. Make a class calendar.

February   2010

SUNDAY	MONDAY	TUESDAY	WEDNESDAY	THURSDAY	FRIDAY	SATURDAY
	1	2	3	4	5	6
7	8	9	10 Lunar New Year	11	12	13
14	15	16	17	18	19	20
21	22	23	24	25	26	27
28						

Have a Holiday Fair

Choose a holiday to research. Make a poster about the holiday. Show decorations used on that day. Display your work and tell about it.

In December, people in many countries celebrate Christmas.

Write an Invitation

Write an invitation to a holiday celebration. When is it? Where is it? What are you celebrating? What will you do?

Dear Friend,
    Please come to my Valentine's Day party. We will share cards and candy.
Date: February 14
Time: 2:00 p.m.
Place: Mrs. Gregory's classroom

Cause and Effect

An **effect** tells what happens. A **cause** tells why it happens. To identify causes and effects:

✔ Ask yourself why things happen.
✔ Look for signal words like *so* and *because*. These words tell what happens and why it happens.

Try the strategy.

from

"This Next New Year"

And . . . Evelyn . . . says Chinese New Year is her favorite holiday because she likes to get red envelopes stuffed with money from her neighbor who came from Singapore.

Why is Evelyn's favorite holiday Chinese New Year? The story says it's because she likes the red envelopes she gets from her neighbor.

Practice

Take this test and identify **causes and effects** in "This Next New Year."

Read each question. Choose the best answer.

1 **The family cleans the house because —**

○ they want to have soup

○ the firecrackers are too loud

○ they want to have good luck

○ they want to wake up the neighbors

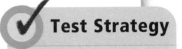

Test Strategy

Think of your own answer. Then see if it is one of the choices.

2 **Because the boy wants to have a fresh start, he —**

○ buys many new clothes

○ does not say bad things

○ does not go to the parade

○ hides when the firecrackers make noise

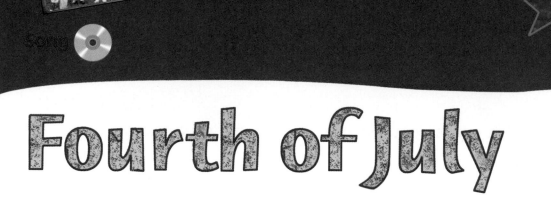

Song

Fourth of July

Our country has a **birthday**, too,

Like yours,

But with a difference.

It's a **celebration** of

Our country's **independence**.

On this day our leaders **signed**

A mighty declaration.

They decided we should all

Have **freedom** for our nation.

—Evelyn Stone

Tune: "Yankee Doodle"

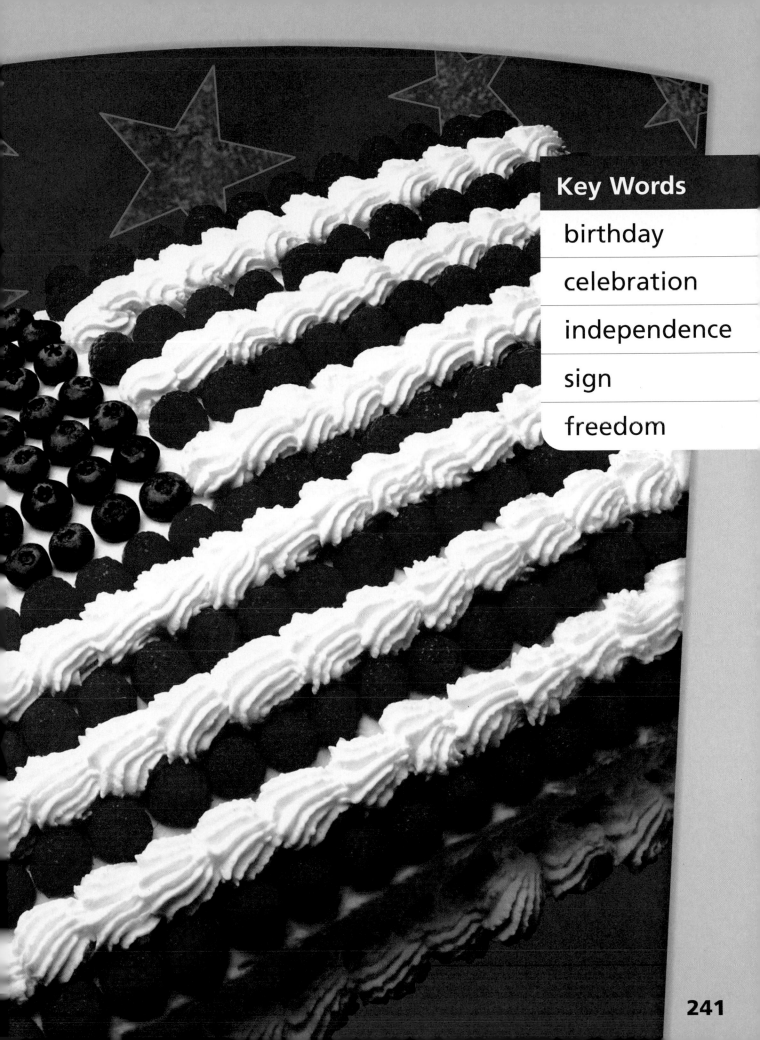

Key Words

birthday

celebration

independence

sign

freedom

241

Read Social Studies

A **social studies article** is nonfiction. It can give facts about people and events today and long ago.

✔ Look for **photos** and **paintings**. Paintings can show life long ago.

▲ photo

▲ painting

Selection Reading

Independence Day

by David F. Marx
illustrated with photographs and paintings

The Fourth of July is the **birthday** of the United States of America. We call this holiday **Independence** Day.

Independence means **freedom**. On Independence Day, we remember when the United States became a free country. That was the **beginning** of the country, or its birthday.

_____

beginning start

▼ **The United States Capitol building in Washington, D.C.**

Before You Move On

1. **Details** When is the birthday of the United States?

2. **Vocabulary** What is another name for the Fourth of July?

More than two hundred years ago, the United States was not yet a country. A king **ruled** the people who lived there. The king was in England, a country **across** the Atlantic Ocean.

_____

ruled led
across on the other side of

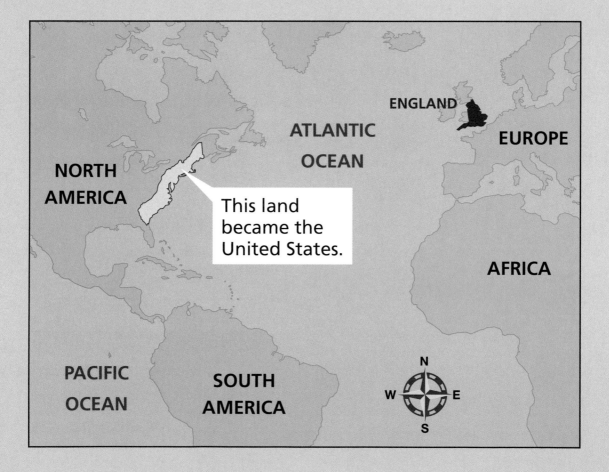

ENGLAND

ATLANTIC
OCEAN

EUROPE

NORTH
AMERICA

This land became the United States.

AFRICA

PACIFIC
OCEAN

SOUTH
AMERICA

N
W E
S

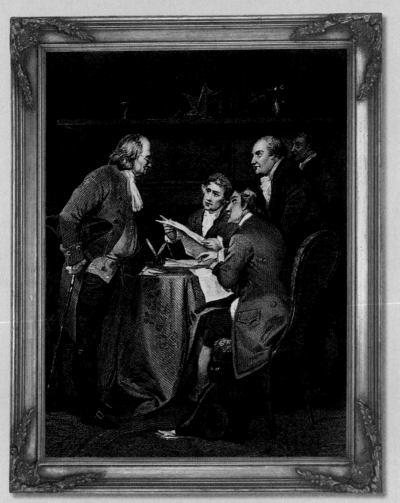

▲ These are some of the men who helped make the United States of America.

In 1776, fifty-six men met in Philadelphia, Pennsylvania. They **agreed** that England should not rule over them. They **decided** that America should be its own country. These men **signed** the Declaration of Independence.

---

agreed all thought
decided said

Before You Move On

1. **Details** What happened in 1776?

2. **Graphic Aid** Name two things the map shows you.

▲ **Thomas Jefferson was the third president of the United States.**

Have you ever heard of Thomas Jefferson?
He wrote the Declaration of Independence.

The Declaration of Independence declared, or said, that the United States of America was free from England.

The Declaration **was dated** July 4, 1776. So the Fourth of July became the birthday of the United States.

_____

was dated showed the date of

▲ The Declaration was written by hand.

Before You Move On

1. **Graphic Aid** When was the Declaration signed?

2. **Inference** Why is July 4 called the birthday of the U.S.?

Every year on Independence Day, Americans celebrate their nation's birthday with huge parties.

The picture below shows a **celebration** from more than one hundred years ago.

▲ **Independence Day in the 1800s**

In some towns, Fourth of July morning starts with a big pancake breakfast.

▲ a Fourth of July pancake breakfast in Anaheim, California

Before You Move On

1. **Details** What do many Americans do every year on Independence Day?

2. **Viewing** Compare the painting and the photo.

Independence Day parties are always decorated in America's special colors: red, white, and blue. These are the colors of the American flag.

Fourth of July meal

Many towns have Independence Day parades. Some people carry American flags as they **march** down the street.

_____

march walk

Fourth of July parade

Before You Move On

1. **Cause/Effect** Why do we see red, white, and blue on July 4?

2. **Viewing** What do the photos show?

The nation's birthday party **lasts** into the night. People gather in parks and **have picnics**. They wait for the sun to **set**.

_____

lasts goes on
have picnics eat food outside
set go down

Then it's time for fireworks! What a great way to end a holiday. Fireworks are pretty, but they are also very loud!

Fireworks are just another way to shout, "Happy Birthday, United States!"

Fireworks at the Statue of Liberty

Before You Move On

1. **Inference** Why do fireworks happen after the sun sets?
2. **Conclusion** Why are there fireworks on the Fourth of July?

Think and Respond

Strategy: Cause and Effect

A **cause** is why something happens. An **effect** is what happens. Make a chart to show why we celebrate the Fourth of July.

Effect		Cause
The Fourth of July is the birthday of the United States	because	it is the day when the United States became a free country.
In 1776, men wrote the Declaration of Independence	because	
We decorate with red, white, and blue	because	
People have breakfasts, parades, picnics, and watch fireworks	because	

Personal Experience

Discuss with a partner what you do to celebrate the Fourth of July.

Talk It Over

1 **Personal Response** What is the most interesting thing you learned from this article?

2 **Comparison** Compare the painting on page 250 to the photograph on page 251. What is the same today and long ago? What is different?

3 **Connect Experiences** Do you know other holidays that are like the Fourth of July? Tell about one.

Compare Topics

Compare how the people in *Day of the Dead* and "Independence Day" celebrate.

All the people make special food.

Content Connections

Take a Vote

large group

Pretend your class can have one celebration this year. What would you celebrate? Give reasons for the one you want. Listen to others' reasons. Then take a vote.

> I vote for a party to celebrate Wednesdays because those are my favorite days!

Make a Class Flag

small group

Talk about what is important to you. Choose one idea. Make a picture, or symbol, to show your idea. Draw your symbol on a flag. Hang the flag in your classroom.

Read Books

Read Books

Read

Research an American Hero

Internet

partners

1. Research the life of a special American.

2. When was the person born? Find other important dates.

3. Make a time line of what happened in the person's life.

George Washington

1732 — George is born.

1759 — George marries Martha.

1789 — George is the first president of the U.S.

Write to Tell How You Feel

on your own

Write something to tell what you do and how you feel on your favorite holiday. You could write:

- a story

- a journal entry.

Does your writing sound like you?

July 4

Today my family had a picnic to celebrate Independence Day. My father told me about living in the U.S. I feel proud to live here. I love my new flag.

Pronouns

Listen and sing.

Song

We Celebrate!

I dance, you dance, so do they.

That's how we celebrate

Until the hour is late.

That's how we celebrate.

She sings, he sings, so do they.

That's how we celebrate.

It is a happy time!

—Joyce McGreevy

Tune: "Down by the Riverside"

How Language Works

A **pronoun** can take the place of a noun.

With a Noun	With a Pronoun
Tran sings.	**He** sings.
The dancers dance.	**They** dance.
The music is loud.	**It** is loud.

Practice with a Partner

Read each sentence. Then say each sentence again.
Use a pronoun for the underlined words.

1. The children march.

2. Sara rides on a float.

3. John and I clap.

4. The parade is over.

One	More Than One
I	we
you	you
he, she, it	they

Put It in Writing!

Write about what you do
on your favorite holiday.
When you edit your work,
check for correct pronouns.

We dance on
Cinco de Mayo.
We have fun.

Show What You Know

Talk About Celebrations

Look back at the pictures. Find one that shows people celebrating. Tell your group what they are doing.

Make a Mind Map

Show what you learned about celebrations.

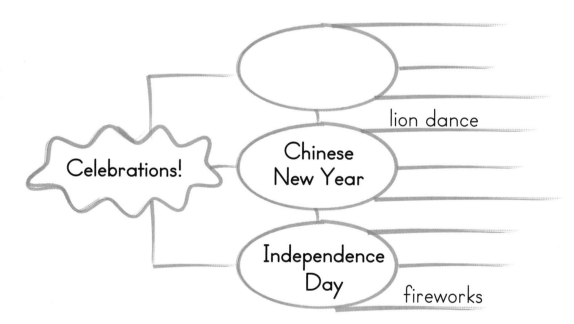

Celebrations!

Chinese New Year — lion dance

Independence Day — fireworks

Think and Write

Write about how you celebrate a holiday. Add this writing to your portfolio.

Read and Learn More

Leveled Books

What a Week!
by Ina Cumpiano

Chinese New Year
by David F. Marx

Theme Library

Celebrating
by Gwenyth Swain

**Apple Pie
4th of July**
by Janet S. Wong

Internet

Go to: www.hbavenues.com

Holiday Clothes

Fourth of July

Birthday Postcards

Catch Me
If You Can

Animal Guessing Game

1. Look at the animal picture on your partner's back.
2. Give your partner clues.
   - What sound does the animal make?
   - How does it move?

Mammals

- Mammals have hair or fur.
- They walk, run, or swim.
- Most are born live.

monkey

bear

Birds

- Birds have feathers.
- They fly, swim, or walk.
- They hatch from eggs.

toucan

eagle

Insects

- Insects have wings, six legs, or both.
- They crawl or fly.
- Most hatch from eggs.

ant

wasp

Fish

- Fish have scales or fins.
- They swim.
- Most hatch from eggs, but some are born live.

red rockfish

clownfish

Reptiles

- Reptiles have scales or shells.
- They crawl, run, or swim.
- Most hatch from eggs.

snake

turtle

Amphibians

- Amphibians have moist skin.
- They swim, hop, or walk.
- Most hatch from eggs.

toad

salamander

Vocabulary

Run and Hide

A **predator** looks for animals to eat. The animals it hunts are called **prey**. Sometimes predators chase their prey. Sometimes they sneak up and **surprise** them. Animals **try hard** to **protect** themselves from predators.

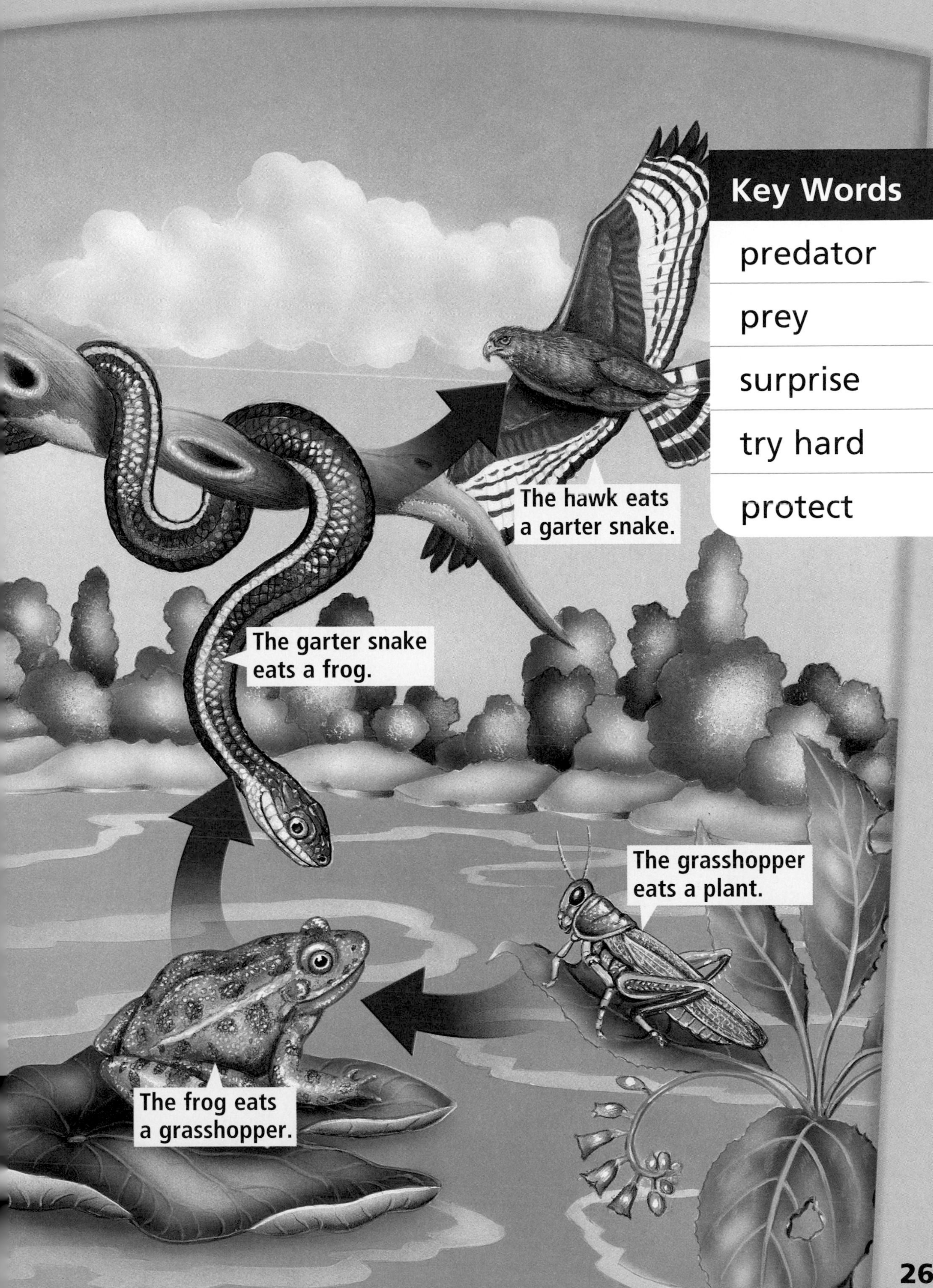

Key Words

predator

prey

surprise

try hard

protect

The hawk eats a garter snake.

The garter snake eats a frog.

The grasshopper eats a plant.

The frog eats a grasshopper.

Read a Science Article

A **science article** gives facts. This article tells you how and why animals do things.

✔ Look at the **pictures.** They help you understand the words.

✔ Look for **labels.** They tell the names of things.

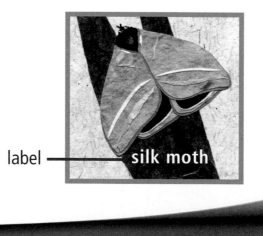

label ———— silk moth

Selection Reading

What Do You Do When Something Wants To Eat You?

adapted from his original book
and illustrated by
Steve Jenkins

Set Your Purpose

What do animals do to protect themselves? Read to find out.

Some animals eat other animals for food. They are **predators**. The animals who get eaten are called **prey**. They **try hard** not to get eaten! Here are some of the ways that animals **protect** themselves from predators.

When an octopus **is threatened** . . .

_____

is threatened could be attacked

fish

octopus

it **squirts** a thick cloud of black ink into the water. This makes the octopus hard to see.

squirts puts

Before You Move On

1. **Main Idea** What is this article about?
2. **Inference** Why is it hard for predators to see the octopus?

W hen this fish is in danger, . . .

puffer fish

barracuda

it **sucks in water** and turns into a big, prickly balloon. This makes the fish **almost impossible** to swallow.

sucks in water takes water into its body

almost impossible very hard

Before You Move On

1. **Judgment** What is the name of this fish? Is it a good name?

2. **Details** Why is this fish hard to swallow?

When it feels threatened, this snake . . .

wolf

hog-nosed snake

rolls onto its back, sticks out its tongue, and plays dead. Most predators do not like to eat animals that they think are already dead.

Before You Move On

1. **Vocabulary** What does it mean to "play dead"?

2. **Cause/Effect** What do predators do when the snake plays dead?

This frog lives in trees in the forests of Asia. It **escapes** predators by . . .

escapes gets away from

gliding frog

green tree snake

webbed feet

using its large webbed feet as wings. This
frog can **glide** as far as fifty feet to reach
another tree.

---

glide fly

Before You Move On

1. **Details** How does the
   frog escape?
2. **Graphic Aid** How
   are the frog's feet
   like wings?

When this moth is in danger, . . .

silk moth

bird

it **spreads** its wings to fly away. **Its attacker** sees two large spots that look like eyes. This **surprises** the predator and gives the moth time to fly away.

spreads opens
Its attacker The predator

Before You Move On
1. **Details** What does the attacker see when the moth spreads its wings?
2. **Cause/Effect** How does this protect the moth?

This insect looks . . .

toad

Javanese
leaf insect

just like a real leaf. The insect's
enemies cannot see it easily.

Before You Move On

1. **Details** How does this
   insect protect itself?

2. **Comparison** How
   is this insect like the
   octopus?

283

This **skink** has a surprise for its attackers.

hawk

blue-tongued skink

skink lizard

It sticks out its large, bright blue tongue and **wiggles** it from side to side. The enemy is surprised and stops attacking for a moment. This gives the skink time to escape.

---

wiggles moves

Before You Move On

1. **Cause/Effect** Why does the skink stick out its tongue?

2. **Details** How does the skink move its tongue?

What would you do if
something wanted to
eat you?

Meet the Author and Illustrator

Steve Jenkins

When **Steve Jenkins** was a child, he collected insects, lizards, mice, and rocks. He also loved to draw and paint. Now Mr. Jenkins makes science books for children. He made the pictures in this article by cutting and gluing special paper.

Before Mr. Jenkins makes an animal picture, he visits the zoo. "I find it useful to see how beautiful they are," he says.

Think and Respond

Strategy: Classify

When you classify, you put things in groups. How do the animals in this article protect themselves? Make a chart. Put each animal in a group.

Ways Animals Protect Themselves	Animals
hide	octopus
get big	
play dead	
escape	

Give an Explanation

Use your own words to tell how animals protect themselves.

Talk It Over

 Personal Response What can you tell a friend about this article?

 Judgment Which animal has the best way of defending itself? Why?

3 **Personal Experience** What animals do you know? How do you think they protect themselves?

Compare Illustrations

Compare the art in this essay to the photos in *Red-Eyed Tree Frog*. How are they the same? How are they different?

Content Connections

Make a Graph

Animals use speed to escape predators or to catch prey. Make a graph of animal speeds. Which animals are the fastest?

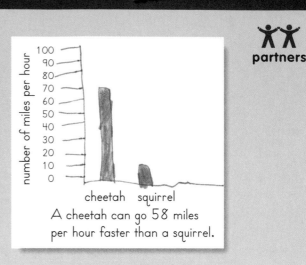

number of miles per hour

100
90
80
70
60
50
40
30
20
10
0

cheetah   squirrel

A cheetah can go 58 miles per hour faster than a squirrel.

partners

Camouflage Experiment

Some animals use their color to escape predators. Play a game to see how camouflage works. Do you think camouflage is a good way for animals to protect themselves?

partners

Play a Guessing Game

Internet

large group

Find an interesting animal.
What kind of covering does
it have? How does it move?
Tell the class about your animal.
Have them guess if your animal
is a mammal, bird, fish, reptile,
insect, or amphibian.

> I am a lion.
> I have fur.

WRITING

Write a Paragraph

on your own

Look back at the science
article. Find two animals.
How do they protect
themselves? Write
a paragraph to
compare them.

The octopus and the puffer fish
both live in the water. They protect
themselves in different ways. The
octopus squirts black ink when
a fish attacks it. Then it hides in the
ink. The puffer fish blows itself up
so the attacker cannot eat it.

Classify

When you **classify**, you put things into groups. Put things in the same group if they are the same in some way.

✔ Think about what group each thing goes in.
✔ Put all of the things that go together in the same group.

Try the strategy.

Where Animals Live

Some animals live in the desert, like lizards and iguanas. Other animals live near the water. Beavers build their homes in ponds. Frogs and turtles live by the water, too.

Frogs, turtles, and beavers go together. They are animals that live by the water.

Practice

Take this test and **classify** words and ideas.

Read the article. Then read the questions. Mark the best answer.

Animals eat different things. Some animals eat plants. For example, sheep and cows eat grass.

Some animals eat other animals. Frogs eat insects. Eagles eat rabbits and other small animals.

Some animals eat plants and animals. Bears eat berries and fish. Chickens eat seeds, but they also eat worms.

1 Look at this chart. It shows what different animals eat.

Eats Only Plants	Eats Only Animals	Eats Plants and Animals
sheep	frog	bear

What animal belongs in the first box?

⬭ bear

⬭ eagle

⬭ cow

⬭ insect

Test Strategy

Do you understand the question? If you don't, read it again.

2 Chicken belongs in the middle box.

⬭ True
⬭ False

Vocabulary

Chant

Smart Move

Don't be **scared**.

Here's what to do

If a **hungry** **enemy**

Wants to eat you!

Protect yourself from

That awful beast.

Here's the **secret**.

Hide underneath

A bigger beast

With bigger teeth!

What a **smart** thing to do!

—Shirleyann Costigan

294

Key Words

scared

hungry

enemy

secret

hide

smart

Grandpa Toad's
SECRETS

**written and illustrated
by Keiko Kasza**

Read a Story

Genre

An **animal fantasy** is a story that shows animals acting like people. In this story, Little Toad learns a lesson from Grandpa Toad.

Characters

Grandpa Toad

Little Toad

Story Problem

Animals want to eat Little Toad and Grandpa Toad.

Selection Reading

1

What is the first secret Grandpa Toad wants to teach Little Toad?

One day Grandpa Toad and Little Toad **took a walk** in the forest.

"You know, Little Toad," said Grandpa, "our world is full of **hungry enemies**."

---

took a walk walked

"How can we protect ourselves, Grandpa?"
asked Little Toad.

"Well," Grandpa **declared**, "I'm going to
share my **secrets** with you. My first secret
is to be brave. You must be brave when
facing a **dangerous** enemy."

---

declared said
facing you meet
dangerous mean

Just then a hungry snake **appeared**.
"Hello, toads," **hissed the snake**.
"I'm going to eat you for lunch!"
 Little Toad screamed and ran away to hide .
But was Grandpa scared ?

—————————

appeared came

hissed the snake the snake said
with a *sss* sound

Not a bit! "Eat me if you can!"
Grandpa shouted **fiercely**. "But I may be more
than you can swallow!"

Grandpa sucked in the air and got bigger
and bigger.

Not a bit! No!
fiercely with anger

"Well," **murmured** the snake, "maybe some other time." And the snake **slithered away**.

_____

murmured whispered
slithered away moved away
on its belly

303

Little Toad jumped from the bushes.
"Oh, Grandpa!" he cried. "You were so brave.
You were wonderful!"

Grandpa Toad **beamed with pleasure**.

"Thank you," he said. "But some enemies are
too big to scare away. My second secret is to
be **smart** . You must be smart when facing
a dangerous enemy."

---

beamed with pleasure smiled

Before You Move On

1. **Goal** What does Grandpa want to teach Little Toad?

2. **Inference** Why does Grandpa suck in air?

Find out how Grandpa Toad tricks his next enemy.

Just then a hungry snapping turtle appeared. "Hello, toads," **snapped the snapper**. "I'm going to **snap you up** for a snack. Snap! Snap!"

Little Toad screamed and ran away to hide. But was Grandpa scared?

_____

snapped the snapper the turtle said
snap you up eat you

Not a bit! "A snack?" asked Grandpa. "Wouldn't you **rather have a feast**?"

"Why, sure," said the snapper.

"Well," Grandpa whispered, "a tasty-looking snake slithered by just moments ago. If you hurry, you can catch him."

"Gee, thanks for the **tip**," said the turtle. And he hurried off to **hunt** the snake.

---

rather have a feast like to have more to eat

tip information

hunt find and eat

Little Toad jumped from the bushes.
"Oh, Grandpa!" he cried. "You were so smart.
You were wonderful!"

Grandpa Toad beamed with pleasure.

"Thank you," he said. "Now, for my third
and last secret." But before he could say
another word . . .

Before You Move On

1. **Comparison** How are the turtle and the snake the same?

2. **Details** What is Grandpa Toad's second secret?

311

3

Find out who wants to eat Grandpa Toad.

A humongous monster appeared.

"Hi, toads," bellowed the monster.

"I'm going to eat you guys just for the fun of it!"

Little Toad screamed and ran away to hide. But was Grandpa scared?

___

humongous monster big make-believe animal

bellowed yelled

you guys both of you

Yes, he was! He had never seen such a **frightening creature** in his life. He tried to run away, but the monster caught him.

---

frightening creature scary animal

315

Little Toad hid in the bushes, shaking with fear. But he **remembered** his grandpa's secrets:

Be brave and be smart!
Be brave and be smart!

He saw some wild berries and quickly decided what to do.

---

remembered thought about

Before You Move On

1. **Cause/Effect** Why is Grandpa Toad afraid of the monster?

2. **Details** What does Little Toad remember?

4 Do you think Little Toad can save Grandpa Toad?

Little Toad threw the berries at the monster. They **splatted** and left red spots all over his legs. The monster didn't even **notice**. He was too busy making Grandpa into a toad sandwich!

---

splatted hit and broke open
notice see

Little Toad stepped bravely out of the bushes. "Grandpa," he yelled, "let that poor monster go!"

"What?" said the monster.

"What?" yelled Grandpa.

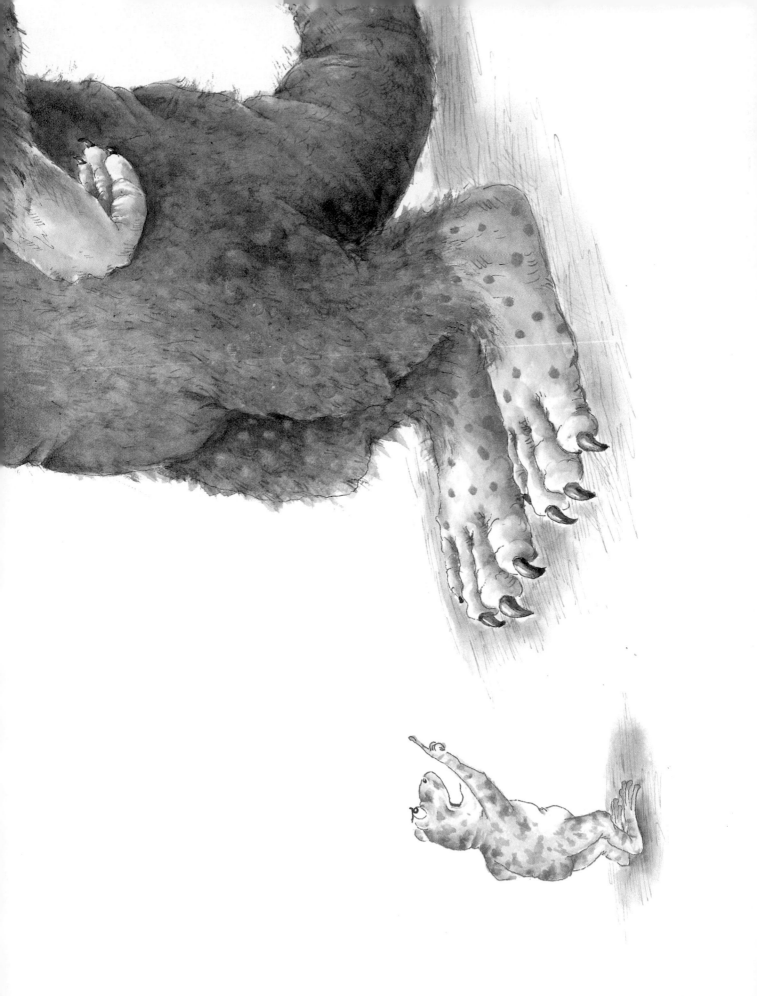

"Grandpa," said Little Toad, "it's not very nice of you to **go around poisoning monsters**. Your poison is already **creeping up** his legs. Soon he'll have spots all over. And then he'll die. **Shame on you**, Grandpa!"

The monster looked at his legs and shouted, "Help! Help! These mean toads are poisoning me!"

---

go around poisoning monsters
make monsters sick
creeping up going up
Shame on you You are bad

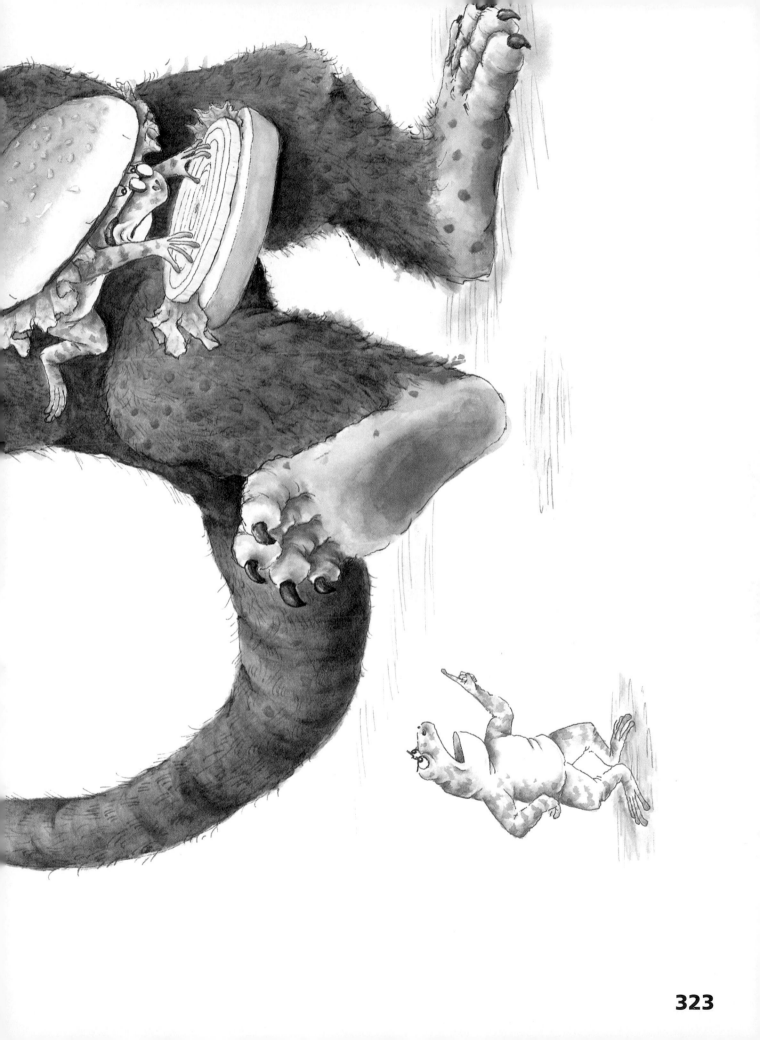

The monster ran away as fast as he could.
Grandpa and Little Toad hugged each other.

"Whew!" sighed Grandpa. "That was
a close call."

"It sure was," said Little Toad.

"Well," said Grandpa finally, "you still
haven't heard my third secret."

"What's that?" asked Little Toad.

a close call scary

"My third secret is this," Grandpa declared. "In case of **emergency**, be sure to have a **friend you can count on**. Little Toad, you were brave. You were smart. You were wonderful!"

Now it was Little Toad who beamed with pleasure.

---

emergency a serious problem

friend you can count on good friend

Before You Move On

1. **Cause/Effect** Why does the monster run away?

2. **Outcome** What does Little Toad learn?

Meet the Author and Illustrator

Keiko Kasza

AWARD WINNER

Keiko Kasza was born in Japan. She grew up on an island with her family.

Ms. Kasza writes and illustrates children's books. When Ms. Kasza writes, she imagines that she is the character, even if it's a pig! "I pretend that I am a bird looking for my mother or a pig trying to impress his girlfriend," she says.

Think and Respond

Strategy: Goal and Outcome

In some stories, the character wants something.
The story tells what the character does to get it.
Make a goal-and-outcome chart for the story.

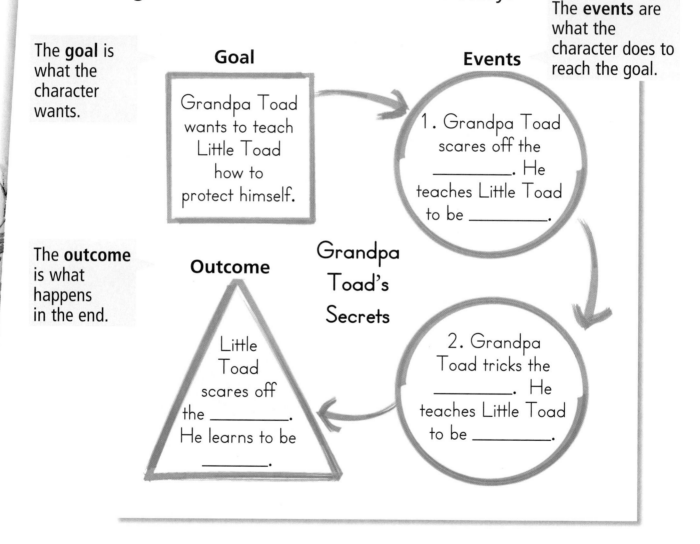

The **goal** is what the character wants.

Goal

Grandpa Toad wants to teach Little Toad how to protect himself.

The **events** are what the character does to reach the goal.

Events

1. Grandpa Toad scares off the _____. He teaches Little Toad to be _____.

The **outcome** is what happens in the end.

Outcome

Little Toad scares off the _____. He learns to be _____.

Grandpa Toad's Secrets

2. Grandpa Toad tricks the _____. He teaches Little Toad to be _____.

Retell

Use your chart to retell the story to a partner.
Does your retelling match your partner's?

Talk It Over

1 **Personal Response** What surprised you in this story?

2 **Judgment** Do you think Little Toad is as smart as Grandpa Toad? Why or why not?

3 **Conclusion** Was Grandpa Toad a good teacher? Why or why not?

Compare Problems

Compare the problems in "Grandpa Toad's Secrets" and "Clever Ana and the Greedy Giant."

In both stories the characters have problems with someone who is very big!

Content Connections

Give Advice

partners

Grandpa Toad gave Little Toad advice. Do you think his advice is good? Is anything important missing from Grandpa's advice? Talk with a partner.

Grandpa Toad should also tell Little Toad to be nice to everyone. Then everyone will be nice to him.

Make an Origami Toad

partners

Origami is a kind of art from Japan. This art is made by folding paper into shapes. Follow the directions to make an origami toad.

Make a Diorama
Internet

Choose an animal.
Find out where it lives.
What is its home like?
Use a shoebox to make
a model of the home.

Write a Story

Imagine that Grandpa Toad and Little
Toad are in the forest again. They meet
a new enemy. Who wants to
eat them this time? Write
a new story. Tell about the
clever way they get away.

Grandpa Toad and Little
Toad meet a cat. They bark
like dogs to scare the cat.

Past Tense Verbs

Listen and sing.

Song

Rabbit and Fox

Here is the story

Of Rabbit and Fox.

Fox looked for food

Underneath the big rocks.

He spotted a rabbit

And asked him to play.

His smile scared the rabbit

Who hip-hopped away.

—Joyce McGreevy

Tune: "Pat-a-Cake, Pat-a-Cake"

How Language Works

A **verb** can change to show when an action happens. Add **–ed** to make a verb tell about the past.

Now	In the Past
1. The toad jumps.	The toad jump**ed**.
2. The foxes walk.	The foxes walk**ed**.

Practice with a Partner

Make each red verb tell about the past. Then say the sentence.

hunt   **1.** A snake _____ in the forest.

move   **2.** It _____ through the grass.

hiss   **3.** It _____ at a little toad.

jump   **4.** The toad _____ onto a branch.

Put It in Writing!

Pretend you saw some animals in a forest. Write a sentence about what they did. When you edit your work, make sure your verbs tell about the past.

The fox followed the rabbit.

333

Show What You Know

Talk About Animals

Look back at the unit. Find one animal.
Tell your group what the animal does
to protect itself.

Make a Mind Map

Show what you learned about animals.

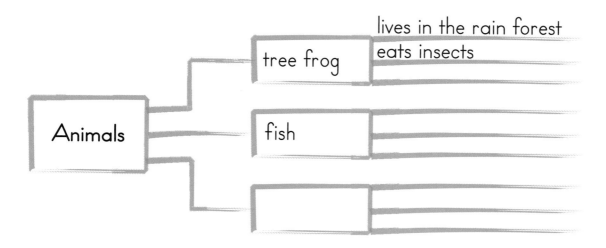

Think and Write

What animal would you like to know more about?
Make a list of questions about that animal. Add
the list to your portfolio.

Read and Learn More

Leveled Books

A Hole Is a Great Home
by Bill Roberts

Hide and Seek
by Evelyn Stone

Theme Library

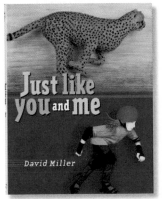

Just Like You and Me
by David Miller

About Amphibians
by Cathryn Sill

Internet

Go to: www.hbavenues.com

Research Animals

Food Chain

Animal Camouflage

Make Some NOISE!

Make Music

1. Make a music maker.
2. Have a class concert.
3. Which sounds were loud, soft, high, and low?

Sound

Loudness

very soft

snowfall

soft

whisper

loud

car horn

very loud

jet

Pitch

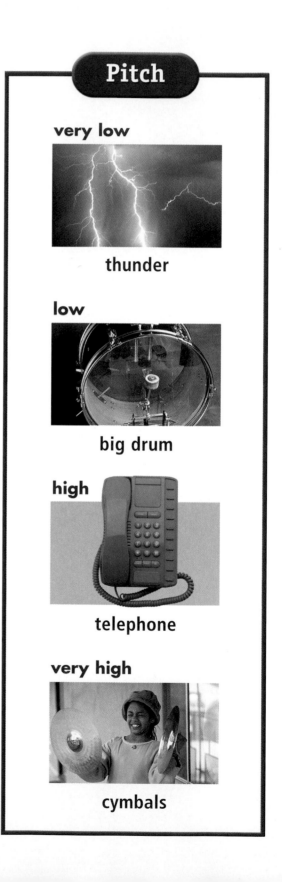

very low

thunder

low

big drum

high

telephone

very high

cymbals

Inventions That Use Sound

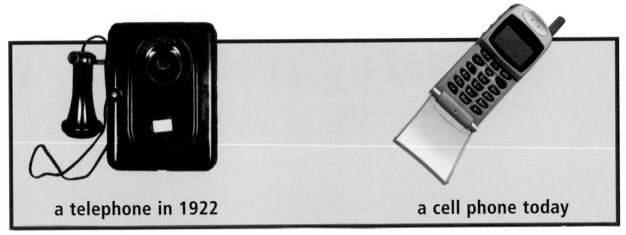

a telephone in 1922

a cell phone today

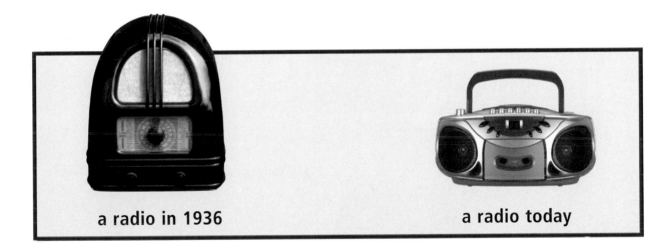

a radio in 1936

a radio today

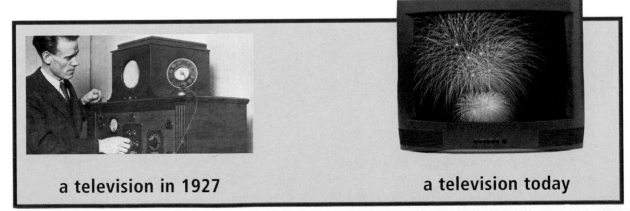

a television in 1927

a television today

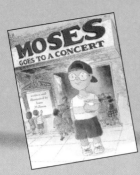

Vocabulary

Ready for the Concert

Pretend you are going on a field trip.
Act out the scenes.

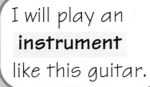

Key Words

concert

field trip

instrument

feel

vibration

341

Read a Story

Genre

This story tells about things that could really happen. It is **realistic fiction** .

Characters

Moses

classmates

Mr. Samuels

Ms. Elwyn

Setting

This story happens at a concert.

▲ orchestra

Selection Reading

1

Find out where Moses and his classmates are going.

I   PLAY   THE DRUM

Moses plays on his new drum.

He can't hear the sounds he is making because he is deaf, but he **feels** the **vibration** of the drum through his hands. He has taken off his shoes so he can feel it through his feet, too.

Today, Moses is going on a **field trip** .
His teacher, Mr. Samuels, is taking him and
his classmates, who are all deaf, to a young
people's **concert** .

As the children climb onto the bus, they
wonder what is inside Mr. Samuels's black bag.

"A big surprise," **signs Mr. Samuels**.

---

wonder try to guess

signs Mr. Samuels says Mr. Samuels
with his hands

THE TEACHER | HAS | A BIG SURPRISE

On the bus, Moses signs to his friend.
"John! My parents gave me a new drum!"
John signs back. "I got one, too!"

MY

FRIEND

Children from all over the city are coming to the concert. Moses and his friend John wait for their class to get off the bus so they can go inside together.

Before You Move On

1. **Character** Who is this story about?

2. **Details** How do Moses and his friend talk to each other?

351

2

Moses meets a musician. What does she play?

Mr. Samuels **leads** them to their seats in the **first row**. Across the stage, in front of the orchestra, are all the percussion **instruments**.

———————

leads takes
first row front

"Children, the percussionist is a friend of mine," signs Mr. Samuels.

"What's a percussionist?" Anna signs back.

"A musician who plays an instrument such as a drum, cymbals, even a piano," replies Mr. Samuels.

A young woman walks onto the stage. Everyone stands up to applaud. Some of Moses's classmates wave instead of clapping. The percussionist smiles and **bows** to the audience.

---

bows bends over

WE WAVE AND APPLAUD

"She has no shoes!" Moses signs in surprise. The teacher smiles and signs, "She is deaf, too. She **follows** the orchestra by feeling the vibrations of the music through her **stocking feet**."

---

follows plays music with
stocking feet feet with socks and no shoes

ELEVEN   BEAUTIFUL   BALLOONS

Then Mr. Samuels takes eleven balloons out of his black bag and hands one to each of his students.

"Oh! What beautiful balloons!" Anna signs.

"Hold them on your laps," signs Mr. Samuels. "They'll help you feel the music."

The conductor turns to **face** the orchestra
and raises **his baton**. The percussionist strikes
the huge gong and the concert begins.

---

face look at

his baton the stick he uses to lead
the orchestra

The percussionist watches the conductor and moves from one instrument to the next, **striking** each to make a sound.

Moses and his classmates hold their balloons in their laps. They can feel the music as their balloons **pick up** the vibrations.

---

striking hitting
pick up move because of

I FEEL VIBRATIONS

Before You Move On

1. **Cause/Effect** Why doesn't the percussionist wear shoes?
2. **Details** How does a balloon help Moses?

3

What do
the students
learn about
Ms. Elwyn?

When the concert is over, Mr. Samuels
has another surprise. He takes the children
onstage to meet his friend, Ms. Marjorie Elwyn.
"She will tell you how she became a
percussionist," signs Mr. Samuels.

_____

onstage onto the stage

"I **became seriously ill** at the age
of seven," signs Ms. Elwyn. "And when I
recovered, I found out that I had lost my
hearing. I was deaf."

"What did you do then?" signs Moses.

---

became seriously ill got very sick
recovered got better

[MY] FRIENDS	AND	I	ARE DEAF

I

WORKED HARD.

MY

HEART

WAS SET ON

BECOMING

A PERCUSSIONIST

AND

I

DID.

_____

MY HEART WAS SET ON BECOMING
I wanted to be

366

"Now you can **play on** my musical instruments," Ms. Elwyn signs. "Come with me, children."

_____

play on make music with

Before You Move On

1. **Goal** What did Ms. Elwyn want to become?

2. **Predict** What will Moses play?

4

What
happens at
the end of
the story?

Anna plays on the marimba. . .
Beverly strikes the triangle. . .

Mark pounds the floor tom and the cymbal. . .
Dianne beats the tom-toms. . .
John hits the snare drum. . .
and Moses thumps the bass drum. . .

David strikes the gong. . .
Tommy and Suzy play on the tubular bells. . .

while Steve bangs the kettledrum and
Maria plays the congas.

"Children! We have to go!" Mr. Samuels
announces after a while. "Ms. Elwyn has to get
ready for another concert."

Moses and his classmates sign thank you,
and they wave goodbye to Ms. Elwyn.

———————————

announces says

THANKS

GOODBYE

On the bus on the way home, Moses signs,
"It was so much fun!"

SO MUCH   FUN

Before You Move On

1. **Details** Name three
   instruments.
2. **Predict** Will Moses
   want to be a
   percussionist? Why do
   you think so?

Isaac Millman

AWARD WINNER

Isaac Millman wrote *Moses Goes to a Concert* because he wanted to have children read about people who use sign language.

Most of Mr. Millman's stories come from real experiences. He says, "Real life is the best inspiration for my stories." Mr. Millman was born in France. He moved to the United States when he was a teenager.

Think and Respond

Strategy: Analyze Story Elements

A story map is a picture of all the parts of a story:
- ✔ the title
- ✔ the setting
- ✔ the characters
- ✔ the plot, or events, in the story.

Make a story map for "Moses Goes to a Concert."

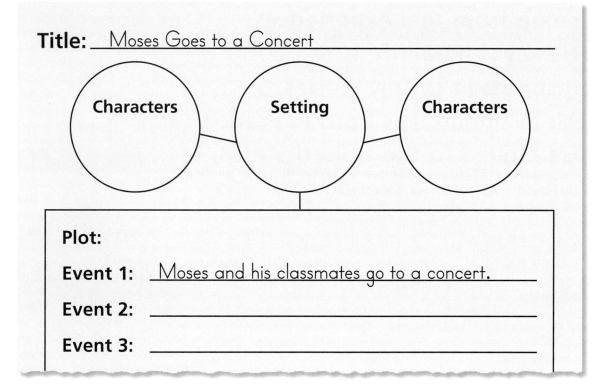

Title: _Moses Goes to a Concert_

Characters   Setting   Characters

Plot:

Event 1: _Moses and his classmates go to a concert._

Event 2: _____

Event 3: _____

Retell the Story

Retell the story. Try to use some sign language in your retelling.

Talk It Over

 Personal Response Pretend that you are at the concert with Moses. Which instrument do you play?

 Inference How do you think Moses feels about music? Why?

3 **Judgment** Does Ms. Elwyn help the class? How? Give examples from the story.

Compare Characters

Compare the boy from "This Next New Year" and Moses. How are they alike? How are they different?

Each of the boys has a dream.

Content Connections

Ask Questions

partners

Choose an instrument you
want to know more about.
Think of some questions.
How would you ask a
friend, a teacher, and
a famous musician?
Practice with a partner.

Ms. Elwyn, could
you please tell
me. . . ?

Experiment with Sound

small group

Put different amounts
of water into four glasses.
Tap the sides of the glasses
with a spoon. Put the glasses
in order, from lowest sound
to highest sound. Draw
a conclusion.

Research an Instrument

partners

Internet

Find out about an instrument. What country is it from? Draw a diagram. Label the parts.

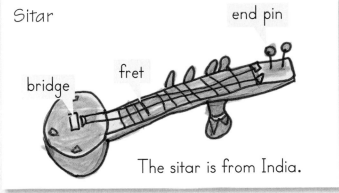

Sitar

end pin

fret

bridge

The sitar is from India.

WRITING

Write to Give Information

on your own

Write about what you want to be when you grow up. Choose the best way to give information:

- a letter

- a paragraph.

Try to use correct spelling, capitalization, punctuation, and grammar.

I want to be a teacher when I grow up. I want to teach children to read and write.

Summarize

A summary tells the important information in what you read. To **summarize** :

✔ Tell the key events.
✔ Don't repeat any information.
✔ Keep your summary short.

Try the strategy. First, make a list of key events in Part 1 of "Moses Goes to a Concert." Then summarize them.

from

"Moses Goes to a Concert"

Today, Moses is going on a field trip. His teacher, Mr. Samuels, is taking him and his classmates, who are all deaf, to a young people's concert.

As the children climb onto the bus, they wonder what is inside Mr. Samuels's black bag.

"A big surprise," signs Mr. Samuels.

> Moses and his classmates are going to a concert. They are all deaf. Their teacher has a surprise for them.

Practice

Take this test and **summarize** "Moses Goes to a Concert."

Read each question. Choose the best answer.

1 Which of these details does <u>not</u> belong in a summary of the story?

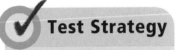

Test Strategy

Look for key words like <u>not</u> and <u>best</u>. They help you find the answer.

- ⬭ The class goes to a concert.
- ⬭ The students feel the music through balloons.
- ⬭ Ms. Elwyn's socks are pink.
- ⬭ The students play the instruments.

2 Read the summary.

> Moses and his classmates are deaf.
> One day they go to a concert.
> _____

Which sentence finishes the summary?

- ⬭ Their teacher is nice.
- ⬭ David plays the gong.
- ⬭ The percussionist's name is Marjorie Elwyn.
- ⬭ They meet a percussionist who is deaf, too.

Sounds

Messages travel

In the sounds you hear,

High sounds and **low** .

We can **measure** the softest

To the **loudest** sound,

As these sounds come

And go.

—Maria Del Rey

Key Words

message

travel

high

low

measure

loudest

Read a Science Article

A **science article** can tell you how things work.

✔ Look at the **graphs**. Graphs help you compare information.

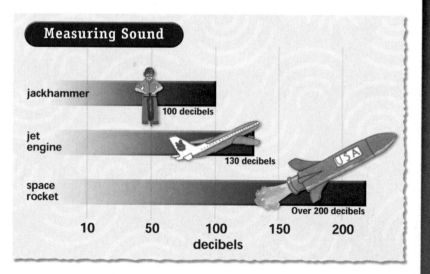

Measuring Sound

jackhammer — 100 decibels

jet engine — 130 decibels

space rocket — Over 200 decibels

10 50 100 150 200
decibels

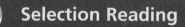 **Selection Reading**

Sounds All Around

by Wendy Pfeffer
illustrated by Holly Keller

Snap your fingers. Clap your hands. Whistle! Clatter some pans. You're making sounds!

Crinkle-crunch through dry leaves.

Splish-splash in a puddle.

384

Shake a can of marbles . . . rattle, rattle, rattle.
Shake a can of pencils . . . clank, clank, clank.
Your sounds fill the air.

Make more sounds. Sing. Talk. Hum. These sounds
come out of your mouth, but they start in your throat.

Before You Move On

1. **Main Idea** What are these pages mostly about?
2. **Details** Name three ways to make sound.

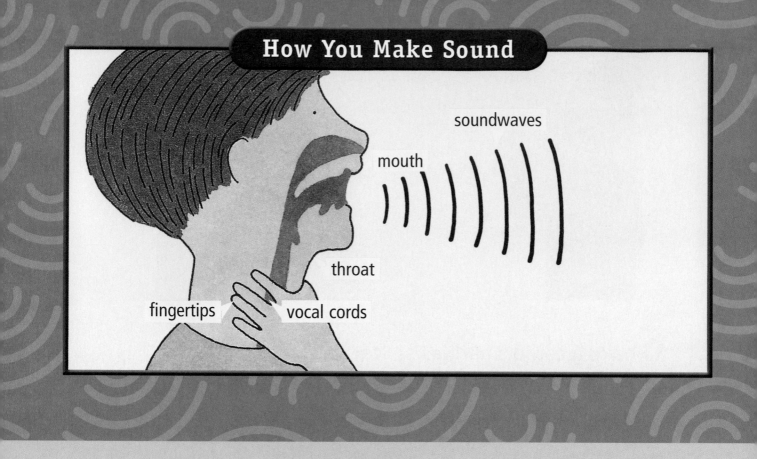

How You Make Sound

Feel your throat as you sing, talk, or hum. Your fingertips **tingle** because your vocal cords shake to make sounds.

They shake back and forth very fast. This is called vibrating. And that makes the air around them vibrate. These vibrations move through the air in waves called sound waves.

———————————

tingle move a tiny bit

Now, be quiet. Feel your throat. Your vocal cords are **still**. When there's no sound, the vocal cords don't vibrate.

---

still quiet, not moving

Before You Move On

1. **Paraphrase** How do you make sound?
2. **Cause/Effect** When something does not vibrate, what happens?

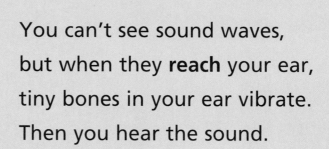

You can't see sound waves,
but when they **reach** your ear,
tiny bones in your ear vibrate.
Then you hear the sound.

_____

reach get to

How You Hear

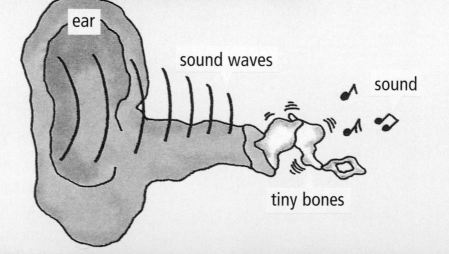

ear

sound waves

sound

tiny bones

Beating a drum makes
it vibrate, and then the air around
it vibrates. These vibrations **ripple**
through the air. They **travel** from
the drum to your ears, and you
hear the sound of the drum.

---

ripple move

Before You Move On

1. **Cause/Effect** What happens when sound waves reach your ear?
2. **Paraphrase** Tell how you hear a drum.

Long ago, people used drum sounds to send **messages**. They beat **high** sounds, **low** sounds, fast sounds, slow sounds. These sounds traveled through the air, from **village to village**. Different **drumbeats** sent different messages.

---

village to village small town to small town
drumbeats sounds made on a drum

These messages could be important news.

"Rain clouds are forming."

"A new leader has been chosen."

Before You Move On

1. **Details** How were drums used to send messages?
2. **Comparison** How do phones and drums send messages differently?

People still use sounds to send messages. Clapping your hands says, "Good job."

CLAP

KNOCK
KNOCK

A knock on the door asks, "Is anyone home?"

And the siren on a fire truck means, "Get out of the way!"

EEEEEEEEEEE

CLUCK, CLUCK, CLUCK

Animals use sounds to send messages, too.
A hen clucks to call her chicks.

HOWWWWL !

A howler monkey
roars to keep other
howlers out of its
territory. A howler's
roar is one of the
loudest animal sounds
in the world. **No wonder**
other howlers stay out
of the way.

---

territory home area
No wonder That is why

Before You Move On

1. **Conclusion** What
   messages can people
   send without talking?
2. **Details** How do
   animals use sound?

Sound is an important part of our lives. Some sounds, like music, **please us**. Some sounds, like a jackhammer, **annoy us**. Some sounds are quiet. Some are loud.

---

please us make us happy
annoy us make us angry

How can you measure sounds?

Weight is how much you weigh.

It is measured in pounds.

65 POUNDS !

54 INCHES !

Height is how tall you are.

It is measured in inches.

80 DECIBELS !

Loudness is how loud you yell.

It is measured in decibels.

Before You Move On

1. **Conclusion** What sounds please people?

2. **Main Idea** How can you measure sound?

▲ whisper

▲ talk

yell ▶

Whispering measures only about 20 decibels. Talking measures about 50 decibels. A loud yell measures about 80 decibels.

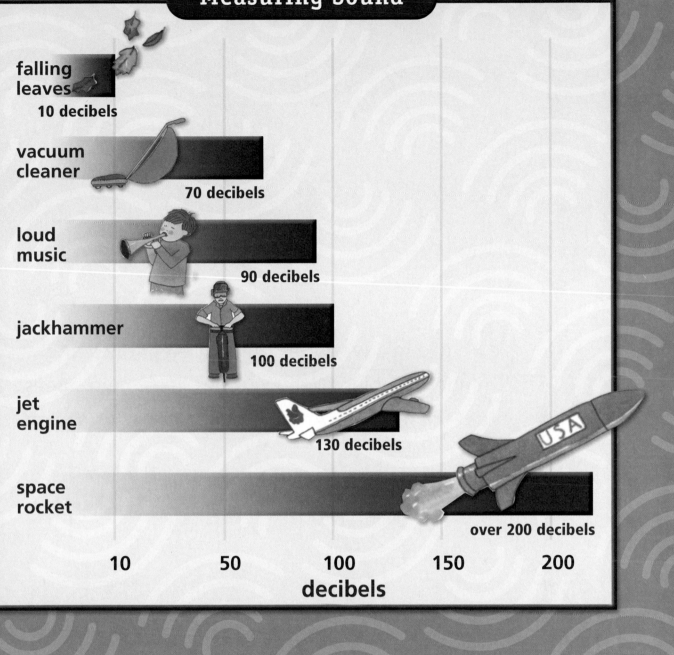

Measuring Sound

- falling leaves — 10 decibels
- vacuum cleaner — 70 decibels
- loud music — 90 decibels
- jackhammer — 100 decibels
- jet engine — 130 decibels
- space rocket — over 200 decibels

10   50   100   150   200
decibels

Some loud sounds can **damage** your ears.
People who are close to airplanes or use
jackhammers should protect their ears.

---

damage hurt

We live in a world of sounds. Telephones ring. Thunder rumbles. Water gurgles. Birds chirp. Bees buzz. Friends talk. And we laugh, cry, hiccup, sigh.

Sounds are all around. Keep listening!

Before You Move On

1. **Graphic Aid** Which sound is the loudest?
2. **Conclusion** What should people do if they are near loud sounds?

Meet the Author

Wendy Pfeffer

AWARD WINNER

Wendy Pfeffer's grandfather was a doctor who loved to tell stories. Her father was a math teacher. Ms. Pfeffer grew up in a household of math and language. Her love of words came from her family.

Even as a child, Ms. Pfeffer wanted to be a writer. The first thing she wrote was her own folk tale. Now she writes nonfiction science books for children.

Think and Respond

Strategy: Main Idea and Details

Main ideas are the most important ideas in an article. Details tell about the main idea.

Pages	Main Ideas	Details
384–385	There are many ways to make sounds.	snap clap whistle shake a can sing talk
386–389		

Complete the chart. Show the main idea and details for each section of the article.

- pages 386–389
- pages 390–393
- pages 394–398

Summarize

Use your completed chart to summarize the article. Tell the main ideas.

Talk It Over

1 **Personal Response** Which part of the article helps you understand sound the best?

2 **Conclusion** Can you send messages with sounds? How?

3 **Comparison** Compare how people and animals send messages.

Compare Genres

"Moses Goes to a Concert" is fiction. "Sounds All Around" is nonfiction. Compare what you learned about sound from each one.

Content Connections

Play the Telephone Game

large group

Sit in a circle. One person whispers a message to the next person. Each person passes it on. The last person says the message out loud. What happened to the message?

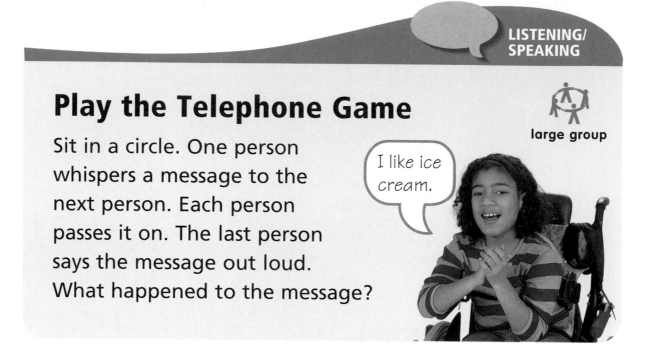

I like ice cream.

Listen to Sounds

small group

What sounds do you hear every day? Who or what makes those sounds? Where do you hear the sounds? Keep a log. Then tell about the sounds in your world.

Who or What	Sound	Where
truck horn	beep	street
bird	chirp	tree

Sound Wave Experiment

Where do sounds seem the loudest? Where do the same sounds seem quieter? Make sounds in different kinds of rooms. Guess what causes the sounds to seem louder or softer.

Write a Safety Newsletter
Internet

Find out about how to take care of your ears or another part of you! Write an article that tells how to be safe. Put it in a class newsletter.

Safety News

The Danger of Loud Music

Be careful not to listen to music that is too loud. It can damage your ears.

Location Words

Listen and sing.

Song 🔘

Night Music

My head's on my pillow,

I am in my bed.

I hear music playing

Inside my sleepy head.

Stars are far above me.

Bear's under my arm.

When I hear the music,

I feel safe and warm.

—Joyce McGreevy

Tune: "Au Claire de la Lune"

How Language Works

Some words can tell where something is.

in	The concert is **in** the park.
on	We sit **on** the grass.
above	The moon is **above** the trees.

Practice with a Partner

Choose the red word that makes sense.
Then say each sentence.

to / at   **1.** We go _____ a party.

by / on   **2.** Loud music plays _____ the radio.

in / from   **3.** We dance _____ the living room.

out / under   **4.** The cat hides _____ the bed.

Put It in Writing!

Write about a noisy place.
Tell about the sounds you
hear there.

I hear loud voices
in the lunchroom.

Show What You Know

Talk About Sound

Look back at the unit. Tell a partner one fact about sound that you learned.

Make a Mind Map

Show what you learned about sounds.

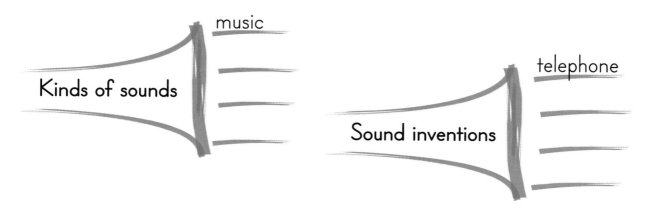

music

Kinds of sounds

telephone

Sound inventions

Think and Write

What makes soft sounds? What makes loud sounds? Make a list of sounds from the softest to the loudest. Add this writing to your portfolio.

Read and Learn More

Leveled Books

Boom Boom Bay!
by Mary Blocksma

Let's Hear It for Ears!
by Shirley Frederick

Theme Library

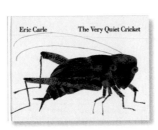

La Cucaracha Martina
by Daniel Moreton

The Very Quiet Cricket
by Eric Carle

Internet

Go to: www.hbavenues.com

World of Music

Make Music

Instrument Fun

Picture Dictionary

The definitions are for the words as they are introduced in the selections in this book.

Pronunciation Key

Say the sample word out loud to hear how to say, or pronounce, the symbol.

Symbols for Consonant Sounds		Symbols for Short Vowel Sounds	Symbols for R-controlled Sounds	Symbols for Variant Vowel Sounds
b box	p pan	a hat	ar barn	ah father
ch chick	r ring	e bell	air chair	aw ball
d dog	s bus	i chick	or corn	oi boy
f fish	sh fish	o box	ur girl	ow mouse
g girl	t hat	u bus	îr fire	oo book
h hat	th Earth			
j jar	th father	**Symbols for Long Vowel Sounds**		**Miscellaneous Symbols**
k cake	v vase	ā cake		shun fraction $\frac{1}{2}$
ks box	w window	ē key		chun question ?
kw queen	wh whale	ī bike		zhun division $2\overline{)100}^{50}$
l bell	y yarn	ō goat		
m mouse	z zipper	ū fruit		
n pan	zh treasure	yū mule		
ng ring				

Parts of an Entry

The **entry** shows how the word is spelled.

rise (rīz)

The sun comes up. Let's watch it **rise!**

The **sample** sentence uses the word in a way that shows its meaning.

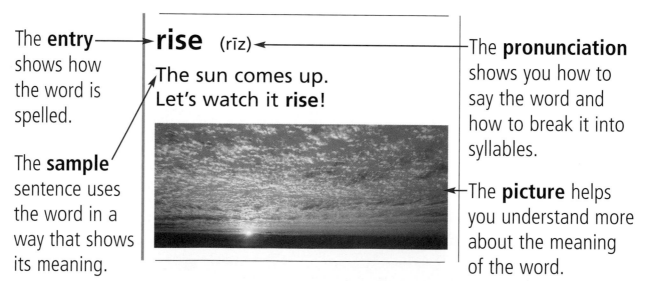

The **pronunciation** shows you how to say the word and how to break it into syllables.

The **picture** helps you understand more about the meaning of the word.

above
(u-**buv**)

Milo is **above** the ground.

afraid
(u-**frād**)

I am **afraid** the book will fall.

arrive   (u-**rīv**)

My grandparents **arrive** for a visit.

suitcase

became
(bē-**kām**)

Look! The caterpillar **became** a butterfly!

caterpillar

butterfly

behind   (bi-**hīnd**)

The dog stays **behind** on the porch.

below
(bi-**lō**)

The yellow and green blocks are **below** the red block.

red

yellow   green

birthday   (**burth**-dā)

Reza has a **birthday** today. He is 8 years old.

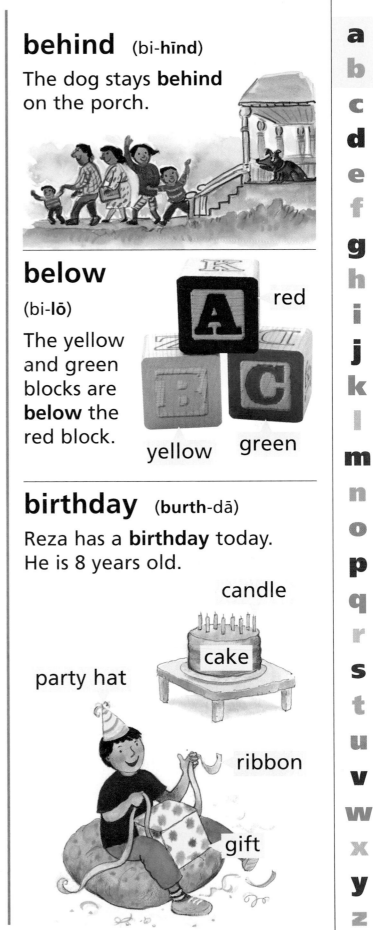

candle

cake

party hat

ribbon

gift

a
b
c
d
e
f
g
h
i
j
k
l
m
n
o
p
q
r
s
t
u
v
w
x
y
z

A B C D E F G H I J K L M N O P Q R S T U V W X Y Z

brave (brāv)

The **brave** knight saves the princess.

dragon

knight

princess

buy (bī)

Lien will **buy** a balloon.

vendor

C

celebration

(sel-u-**brā**-shun)

We give gifts at our **celebration**.

gift

clever (klev-ur)

This **clever** cat can open the door!

cloud (klowd)

Look up at the sky. Can you see a **cloud**?

cloud   sky

concert (kon-surt)

At a **concert**, you listen to music.

crowded (krowd-ed)

The street is **crowded**.
There are a lot of people.

dairy

(dair-ē)

Cheese, ice cream, and milk are **dairy** foods. Dairy foods come from cows.

cheese

milk

ice cream

disappear (dis-u-pir)

The magician made the ball **disappear**.

ball   magician

dream (drēm)

❶ Rob has a **dream**.
What is your dream?

❷ You **dream** when you sleep.

enemy

(en-u-mē)

This lion is the **enemy** of the zebra.

lion   zebra

envelope

(en-vu-lōp)

The card came in an **envelope**.

card   stamp

envelope

A
B
C
D
E
F
G
H
I
J
K
L
M
N
O
P
Q
R
S
T
U
V
W
X
Y
Z

everywhere

(ev-rē-**whair**)

Flowers are **everywhere**! They are all around me.

factory

(**fak**-tur-ē)

People work with machines in a **factory**. They make products.

farming

(**farm**-ing)

This man's job is **farming**.

farmer   tractor

plow

field

favorite   (fā-vur-it)

Viv likes this book best. It is her **favorite** book.

feel   (fēl)

Feel this snowball. It's cold!

snowball

field trip   (fēld trip)

This class is on a **field trip** to the zoo.

flow   (flō)

These rivers **flow** into the ocean.

ocean

river

freedom (frē-dum)

She gives the bird its **freedom**.

friend

(frend)

Suzu is Hana's **friend**. Hana is Suzu's friend.

G

give away

(giv u-**wā**)

They **give away** their old clothes.

ground

(grownd)

We plant seeds in the **ground**.

grow (grō)

How does a plant **grow**?

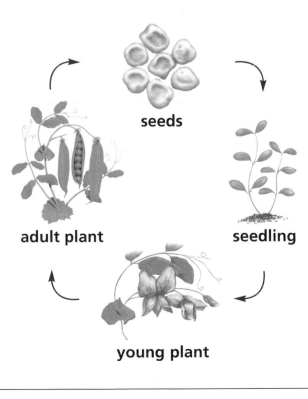

seeds

adult plant

seedling

young plant

A B C D E F G H I J K L M N O P Q R S T U V W X Y Z

H

hide (hīd)

The tiger can **hide** in the grass.

high (hī)

This woman sings a **high** note.

holiday (hol-u-dā)

Thanksgiving is a special day. It is a **holiday**.

hungry (hung-rē)

Is it time to eat? I am **hungry**!

napkin

glass

plate

I

idea

(ī-**dē**-u)

What a good **idea**!

in between (in bi-**twēn**)

The snowman is **in between** Noor and Jack.

independence

(**in**-di-**pen**-duns)

This bird can fly alone now. It has **independence**.

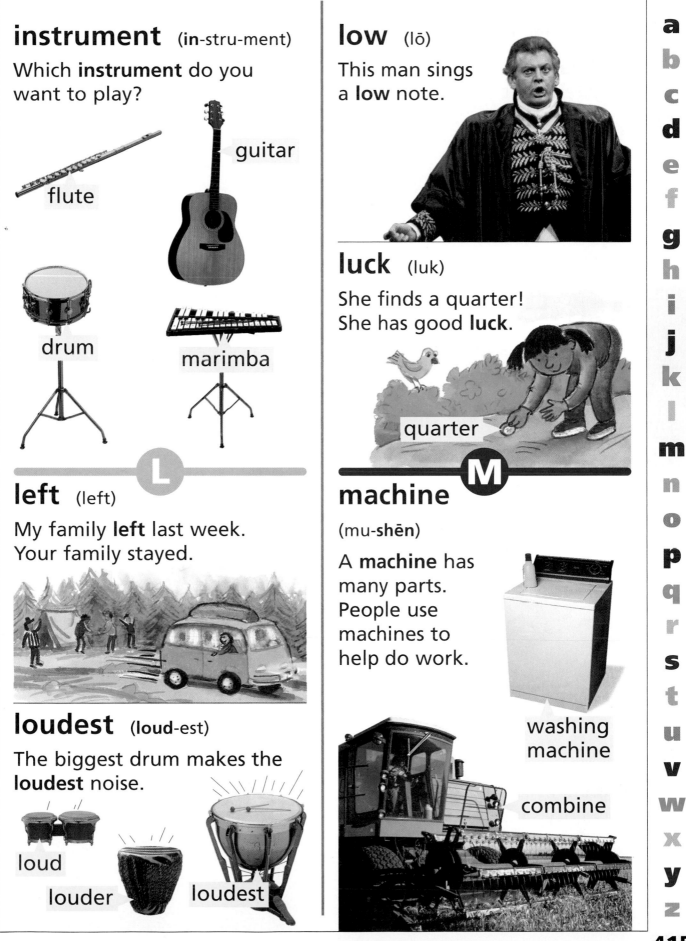

instrument (in-stru-ment)

Which **instrument** do you want to play?

flute

guitar

drum

marimba

L

left (left)

My family **left** last week. Your family stayed.

loudest (loud-est)

The biggest drum makes the **loudest** noise.

loud

louder

loudest

low (lō)

This man sings a **low** note.

luck (luk)

She finds a quarter! She has good **luck**.

quarter

M

machine

(mu-shēn)

A **machine** has many parts. People use machines to help do work.

washing machine

combine

a b c d e f g h i j k l m n o p q r s t u v w x y z

415

market (mar-kit)

You can buy fruits and vegetables at the **market**.

measure (mezh-ur)

This machine can **measure** sound.

message (mes-ij)

Luis reads a **message** from Mom.

message

neighbor (nā-bur)

Brenna lives near Quincy. She is Quincy's **neighbor**.

neighborhood (nā-bur-hood)

People live and work in a **neighborhood**.

noisy (noi-zē)

Juan's trumpet is **noisy**.

predator (pred-u-tur)

A shark is a **predator**. It hunts and eats other fish.

shark

prey (prā)

Will the shark catch its **prey**?

product (praw-dukt)

Wood is a **product** from a tree.

protect

(pru-**tekt**)

A helmet can **protect** your head.

helmet

elbow pad

knee pad

puddle

(**pud**-ul)

He splashes in the **puddle**.

puddle

R

restaurant (**res**-tur-ahnt)

We like to eat at a **restaurant**.

rise (rīz)

The sun comes up. Let's watch it **rise**!

S

save (sāv)

His neighbor will **save** him from the cold water.

scared

(skaird)

The elephant is **scared** of the mouse!

secret

(sē-krit)

You can tell a friend a **secret**.

a b c d e f g h i j k l m n o p q r s t u v w x y z

A B C D E F G H I J K L M N O P Q R S T U V W X Y Z

sign (sīn)

Bev can **sign** her name.

pen

paper

smart (smart)

Kee is **smart**. He puts his books in a backpack.

surprise (sur-prīz)

I will **surprise** Kendra.

T

travel

(trav-ul)

Music can **travel** across the park. Tasha hears the music.

trouble (trub-ul)

Look at all the **trouble** he has!

try hard (trī hard)

She will **try hard** to ride the bicycle.

V

vegetable (vej-tu-bul)

A **vegetable** is a healthy food.

carrot

radishes

potatoes

vibration

(vī-**brā**-shun)

The jackhammer shakes a lot. The worker feels each **vibration**.

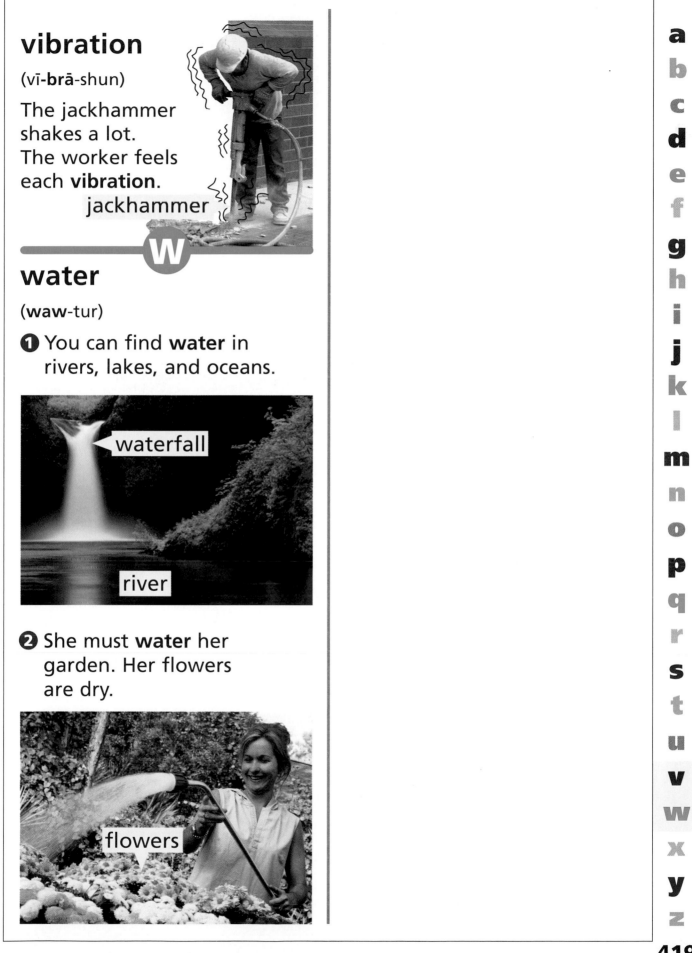

jackhammer

water

(**waw**-tur)

❶ You can find **water** in rivers, lakes, and oceans.

waterfall

river

❷ She must **water** her garden. Her flowers are dry.

flowers

Acknowledgments continued

Children's Press: *Where Do Puddles Go?* by Fay Robinson. © 2001 Children's Press ® A Division of Grolier Publishing Co., Inc. All rights reserved. *Independence Day* by David F. Marx. © 2001 Children's Press ® A Division of Grolier Publishing Co., Inc. All rights reserved.

Farrar, Straus and Giroux, LLC: *Moses Goes to a Concert* by Isaac Millman. Copyright © 1998 by Isaac Millman. Reprinted by permission of Farrar, Straus and Giroux, LLC. *This Next New Year* by Janet S. Wong, pictures by Yangsook Choi. Text copyright © 2000 by Janet S. Wong. Pictures copyright © 2000 by Yangsook Choi. Reprinted by permission of Farrar, Straus and Giroux, LLC.

G.P. Putnam's Sons: *Grandpa Toad's Secrets* by Keiko Kasza. Copyright © Keiko Kasza, 1995. Published by arrangement with G.P. Putnam's Sons, an imprint of Penguin Putnam Books for Young Readers, a divison of Penguin Putnam Inc. All rights reserved.

Grasset & Fasquelle: *Eva's Cloud.* Originally published as *L'Histoire du nuage qui était l'ami d'une petite fille* © texte et illustrations: Grasset & Fasquelle, 1973. Concept editorial: Francois Ruy-Vidal.

HarperCollins Publishers: *Sounds All Around.* Text copyright © 1999 by Wendy Pfeffer. Illustrations copyright © 1999 by Holly Keller. Used by permission of HarperCollins Publishers.

Henry Holt and Company, LLC: *Chinatown* by William Low, © 1997 by William Low. Reprinted by permission of Henry Holt and Company, LLC.

Houghton Mifflin Company: *What Do You Do When Something Wants To Eat You?* by Steve Jenkins. Copyright © 1997 by Steve Jenkins. Adapted and reprinted by permission of Houghton Mifflin Company. All rights reserved.

Alfred A. Knopf, a division of Random House, Inc: "City" from *The Collected Poems of Langston Hughes* by Langston Hughes, copyright © 1994 by The Estate of Langston Hughes. Used by permission of Alfred A. Knopf, a division of Random House, Inc.

Cedric McClester: "Kwanzaa Is" by Cedric McClester.

Diane Margolis: "Rosh Ha-Shanah Eve" by Harry Philip. From *Poems for Jewish Holidays* selected by Myra Cohn Livingston. All rights reserved. © 1986 Harry Philip. Reprinted by permission of Diane Margolis on behalf of Richard J. Margolis.

Photographs:

p416: courtesy of Brookhaven National Library (measure).

AGStockUSA: p111 (broccoli harvest, © Ed Young), p111 (lettuce harvest, © Tony Hertz), pp122-123 (factory, © David Thurber).

Animals Animals/Earth Scenes: p149 (fair clouds, © Eastcott/Momatiuk), p149 (sunny clouds, © John Lemker), p154 (snowstorm, © Brina Milne).

AP Wide World Photos: p196 (parade, © R.J. Oriez).

Bruce Coleman, Inc.: p267 (salamander, © Gary Meszaros), p267 (toad, © Janis Burger), p293 (snake, © M.P.L. Fogden), p266 (toucan, © Norman Owen Tomalin).

CORBIS: (all © CORBIS) p7, p105 (harvest, © Ron Watts), p65 (portrait), p81 (Chile farm, © Douglas Peebles), p97 (man in window, © AFP), p102 and p125 (rice, © Paul A. Sounders), p104 (milking cow, © Arthur Rothstein), p106 and p124 (artichokes, © Ed Young), p109 (picking corn, © SABA/James Leynse), pp116-117 (wheat field, © Craig Tuttle), p124 (picking tea leaves, © Michael S. Lewis), p125 (picked olives, © Annie Griffiths Belt), p165 (dry terrain, © Adrian Arbib), pp194-195 (boys, © Kevin R. Morris), p196 (Carnaval, © Stephanie Maze), p197 (Thailand, © Reuters New Media Inc.), p198 (trumpet, © Ronnie Kaufman), p198 (cell phone), pp240-241 (flag cake, © Charles Gold), p240 and p242 (kids celebrating, © Ariel Skelley), p242 and p250 (engraving), p243 (celebrating July 4, © Ariel Skelley), p248 (Jefferson, © Bettmann), p252 (meal, © Ariel Skelley), pp252-253 (flag, © Digital Stock), p253 (parade, © Ariel Skelley), p266 (eagle, © Digital Stock), p267 (rockfish, © Digital Stock), p268 (bear, © W. Perry Conway), p338 (jet, © David Lawrence), p338 (snow, © Kevin Fleming), p338 (lightning, © Digital Stock), p339 (1927 TV, © Bettmann), p411 (crowded, © Bill Ross), p413 (give away), p415 (low © Robbie Jack), p419 (waterfall, © Digital Stock).

Getty Images, Inc.: (all © Getty Images) p4 and pp10-11 (city, © Bob Stefko), p6 and pp136-137 (waterfall, © Alan Smith), p8 and pp264-265 (chameleon, © JH Pete Carmichael/The Image Bank), pp12-13 (city, © Sally Beyer/Stone), p43 (store fronts, © Rich LaSalle/Stone), p105 (factory, © Chris Salvo/Taxi), p108 (field, © PhotoDisc), p109 (combine, © PhotoDisc), p110 (peas, pod, broccoli, carrots, tomato and lettuce, © PhotoDisc), p112 (glass of milk, © Artville), p117 (bread, © C Squared Studios), p117 (noodles, © PhotoDisc), p120 (orange, © PhotoDisc), p120 (picking oranges, © Andy Sacks/Stone), p122 (grapefruit, lime, lemon and orange, © Artville), p126 (water can, © PhotoDisc and ear of corn, © Artville), p134 (tomato, © PhotoDisc), p149 (dark clouds, © PhotoDisc), p249 (quill, © PhotoDisc), p249 (declaration, © Hulton Archive), p254 (family, © PhotoDisc), p265 (duck, © PhotoDisc), p265 (lion, © Joseph Van Os), p266 (ant and wasp, © Artville), p266 (bear and monkey, © PhotoDisc), p267 (snake and turtle, © PhotoDisc), p267 (clownfish, © Cousteau Society/The Image Bank), p338 (honk, © J.P.Fruchet/Taxi), p339 (cell phone, © Ryan McVay), p339 (telephone, © Hulton Archive), p339 (TV and fireworks, © PhotoDisc), p343 (symphony, © Barros & Barros/The Image Bank), p408 and p417 (rise, © Digital Vision), p410 (cloud, © PhotoDisc), p411 (enemy, © S Purdy Matthews/Stone), p411 (cheese, © PhotoDisc), p411 (milk and ice cream, © Artville), p412 (everywhere, © Jim Cummins/Taxi), p413 (friend, © PhotoDisc), p414 (high, © Ken Tannenbaum/The Image Bank), p414 (holiday, © Ryan McVay/ PhotoDisc), p415 (instrument and loudest, © Artville), p415 (combine, © PhotoDisc), p418 (vegetable, © PhotoDisc), p419 (woman, © Eyewire).

Grant Heilman Photography, Inc.: p5 and p112 (cow, © Michael O'Neill), p106 (cow, © Larry Lefever), p108 (corn, © Barry Runk/Stan), p113 (cow, © Grant Heilman), p116 (wheat, © Grant Heilman).

ImageState: p410 (celebration, © Patrick Ramsey), p416 (predator, © First Light).

Index Stock: p7 and p255 (fireworks, © Sandra Baker), p13 (taxi, © Image Port), p104, pp106-107, pp128-129 and pp130-131 (farm, © Russell Burden), pp244-245 (capitol, © Michael Howell).

Metaphotos: p409 (below).

New Century Graphics: p117 (tortillas and cereal), p126 (sponge, cup, kernels and pot), p137 (jar), p195 (crown), p199 (stamp), p337 (plastic bottle), p339 (radio).

North Wind Picture Archives: p247 (Washington).

PhotoEdit, Inc.: p13 (train, © Amy Etra), p109 (tractor, © Dennis MacDonald), p124 (bananas, © Jonathan Nourok), p201 (parade, © David Young-Wolff), p242 and p251 (pancake breakfast, © Tony Freeman), p338 (drum, © Amy Etra), p338 and p403 (girl, © David Young-Wolff), p413 (ground, © David Young-Wolff), p415 (washing, © Michael Newman), p417 (protect, © Myrleen Ferguson Cate), p419 (vibration, © Michael Newman).

Photo Researchers, Inc.: p414 (hide, © Stan Wayman).

PictureQuest: (all © PictureQuest) p13 (bus, © John Elk III/Stock, Boston Inc.), p13 (truck, © Sovfoto/ Eastfoto), pp150-151 (stream, © CORBIS Images), p154 (waterfall, © Henryk T. Kaiser, Rex Intstock/Stock Connection), p154 (orca, © Tom Soucek/Alaskan Express), p196 (girl on donkey, © Pete Menze/Stock, Boston Inc.), p197 (festival, © V. Matytsin/Sovfoto/ Eastfoto), p292 (beaver, © Jeff Foott), p416 (prey, © Rainbow).

Science Photo Library: p339 (radio, © Francoise Sauze).

Stockbyte: p338 (telephone).

Superstock, Inc.: p104 (store), p410 (concert), p412 (flow).

The Image Works: p197 (Ramadan, © Carol Beckwith & Angela Fisher/HAGA), p197 (Afahye, © Petcr Sanders /HAGA).

Tony Stone Images: p417 (restaurant, © Rick Rushing).

Tracy Wheeler: p409 (above).

Liz Garza Williams: p5 and pp74-75 (lunch), p6 and p192 (girl), p9 (boy), p11, p75, p195 and p265 (hand), p12 (crosswalk), p36 (girl), p38 (girl), p67 (girl), p68 (boy), p76 (holding seeds), p77 (girl), p79 (kids), p100 (girl), p102 (boy), p123 (girl), p129 (girl), p131(boy), p137 (hand and ice), p140 and pp142-143 (boy), p144 (wet), p145 (dry), p155 (girl and puddle), p157 (boy), p158 (girl), p160 (girl), p160 (boy), p162 (girl), p163 (girl), p188 (kids), p236 (boy), p238 (boy), p257 (boy), p258 (boy), p286 (girl), p290 (paper and hand), p291 (girl), p292 (girl), p329 (girl), p330 (boy), p336 (kids), p337 (hand and drum), p338(kids), p375 (girl), p376 (girls), p378 (girl), p402 (girl), p411 (envelope), p412 (favorite), p416 (market and noisy), p417 (puddle and secret), p418 (sign and try hard).

Author and Illustrator Photos:

p63 courtesy of William Low, p97 courtesy of Lada Kratky, p185 courtesy of Enrique O. Sánchez, p287 courtesy of Steve Jenkins, p373 courtesy of Isaac Millman, p399 courtesy of Wendy Pfeffer.

Illustrations:

Joy Allen: pp140-141 (puddles); **Martha Avilés:** p132 (market); **Doug Bekke:** p413 (grow), **Annie Bissett:** pp76-77 (seed to you), p81 (Chile map), p106 (world), pp114-115 (cow to you), pp118-119 (field to factory), p121 (oranges), p124 (world), pp124-125 (farm world map), p188 (U.S.), pp196-197 (world map), p246 (England map); **Yangsook Choi:** p198, pp201-237 and p262 (*This Next New Year*); **Eva Vagreti Cockrille:** p161 (bucket); **Lynne Cravath:** p70 (park); **Drew Brook-Cormack:** p412 (farming), **Elizabeth Gómez:** p4, pp14-35 and p38 (*A Movie in My Pillow*); **Peter Grosshauser:** p332 (fox and bunny); **Keiko Kasza:** p8, pp294-331 (*Grandpa Toad's Secrets*); **Holly Keller:** p9, pp380-398, p401 and p407 (*Sounds All Around*); **Grace Lin:** pp40 41 (café); **William Low:** p4, pp40-69 (*Chinatown*); **Steve Jenkins:** p8, pp270-291 and p334 (*What Do You Do When Something Wants To Eat You?*); **Barbara Johansen Newman:** pp380-381 (neighborhood); **Cheryl Mendenhall:** p340 (teacher and kids), p341 (playing instruments); **Isaac Millman:** p9, pp340-377 and p406 (*Moses Goes to a Concert*); **Paul Mirocha:** p126 (*How to Grow Corn*), p127 (corn and stalk), pp138-139 (land and water), p142 (evaporation), pp146-147 (evaporation), p148 (evaporation), pp152-153 (water cycle); **Cyd Moore:** pp64-65 (city), p72 (vendor), p190 (dark clouds); **Julie Paschkis:** p229 (author); **Enrique O. Sánchez:** p6, pp162-189 and p193 (*Eva's Cloud*); **Roni Shepherd:** p409 (afraid, arrive, behind, and birthday), p410 (brave, buy, and clever), p411 (disappear and dream), p412 (factory, feel, and field trip), p413 (freedom), p414 (hungry, idea, in between, and independence), p415 (left and luck), p416 (message, neighbor, neighborhood), p417 (product, save, and scared), p418 (smart, surprise, travel, and trouble); **Michael Slack:** pp294-295 (dragon, hog, and mouse); **Rosiland Solomon:** pp268-269 (food chain), p409 (became); **Gerardo Suzán:** p260, p263 (celebration), p404 (fiddler); **Lane Yerkes:** p5, p78, pp80-99, p101 and p135 (*Clever Ana and the Greedy Giant*); **Anne Wilson:** pp14-15 (neighborhood), pp230-231 (moon dance); **Kris Wiltse:** p7 and p232 (Kwanzaa Is), p233 (candle).

The Avenues Development Team

Hampton-Brown extends special thanks to the following staff who contributed so much to the creation of the Grade 1 and 2 Pupil Editions.

Editorial: Renee Biermann, Susan Buntrock, Julie Cason, Honor Cline, Shirleyann Costigan, Roseann Erwin, Kristin FitzPatrick, Margot Hanis, Mary Hawley, Fredrick Ignacio, Phillip Kennedy, Dawn Liseth, Sheron Long, and Ann Seivert.

Design and Production: Chaos Factory and Associates, Kim Cockrum, Sherry Corley, Darius Detwiler, Jeri Gibson, Raymond Ortiz Godfrey, Delaina Hodgden, Raymond Hoffmeyer, Rick Holcomb, Leslie McDonald, Michael Moore, Andrea Pastrano-Tamez, Stephanie Rice, Augustine Rivera, Debbie Saxton, Curtis Spitler, Jonni Stains, Alicia Sternberg, Debbie Wright Swisher, Andrea Erin Thompson, Terry Taylor, Teri Wilson, and Hoshin Woo.

Permissions: Barbara Mathewson.